THE MEDIEVAL

ACCESSUS AD AUCTORES

THE
MEDIEVAL
ACCESSUS
AD AUCTORES

Edwin A. Quain, s.j.

New York
FORDHAM UNIVERSITY PRESS
1986

Printed in the United States of America

CONTENTS

CHARTS

This work has become a classic of its genre. It also remains the only work precisely of its kind, providing a general introduction to the *accessus*, while considering the use of the *accessus* in various disciplines. Medieval commentators on classical authors had a custom of prefixing to their works an introductory summary on the subject of the commentary. This schema comprised all or some of these topics: *vita auctoris, titulus operis, intentio scribentis, materia operis, utilitas*, and *cui parti philosophiae supponatur*. This introductory summary has come to be known as the *accessus ad auctores*, whether or not a particular *accessus* covers all the possible topics.

'Quain's *Accessus*' considers the disciplines of medieval literature, philosophy, rhetoric, and civil and canon law, with additional notice of theology and scriptural exegesis. It forms a necessary prolegomenon to such critical studies as R. B. C. Huygens' *Accessus ad auctores* (Brussels: Latomus, 1954), *Conrad de Hirsau: Dialogus super Auctores* (Brussels: Latomus, 1955), and *Accessus ad Auctores: Bernard d'Utrecht, Bernard d'Hirsau, Dialogus super Auctores* (Leiden: Brill, 1970). It is regularly cited in the literature and, more than four decades since its original publication, seems likely to endure. Even though we publish *Traditio*—indeed, we can still supply copies of Volume III from stock—we believe that 'Quain's *Accessus*' grows less easily found with the passing years. So it seems good to us to make separately available this instrument of research, and to take the opportunity to correct a few typographic errors.

EDWIN A. QUAIN, S.J. (1906–1975), late Professor of Classical Languages and Literature at Fordham University, led an extremely productive academic and administrative life, including the presidency of two other universities. He was, moreover, Director of Fordham University Press from 1956 to 1972, an Editor from 1947 until his death, and an Editor of *Traditio* from 1950 until his death. So his old colleagues are most pleased to have overseen the reissue of this witness to his scholarship.

Canisius Hall
6 IV 1986

THE MEDIEVAL

ACCESSUS AD AUCTORES

The custom of medieval commentators on classical authors of prefixing to their works a *schema* generally called an *accessus* has long been known.[1] In such a prefatory note they treated of items such as the following: *vita auctoris, titulus operis, intentio scribentis, materia operis, utilitas,* and *cui parti philosophiae supponatur.* In different works the number of these items might be curtailed or expanded, but the common purpose of providing an introductory summary to the work in question, is present in all forms of the *accessus.*

This medieval practice has been noticed by specialists in several branches of the studies of the times, and it often appears that the writers have been unaware of the fact that the practice was used in disciplines other than their own. Thus we find mention of it in historians of medieval literature, philosophy, rhetoric, and law, both civil and canon.[2] A complete examination of the subject has not yet been made. This paper will be an attempt to broaden the horizons of the discussion by gathering the available evidence from as many branches of medieval learning as is possible, with a view to placing the matter in its proper perspective, and of clearing up some misconceptions that were inevitable, granted the limited purview of much of the previous work on the subject. Thus attempts have been made to determine the origin of the *accessus,* using

---

[1] The first mention of the *accessus* by a modern scholar is that of Sebastian Gunther, *Geschichte der litterarischen Anstalten in Baiern* (München 1810) I, 271: 'Ich habe mehrere solche Auslegungen gesehen, die grossentheils die Aufschrift führten: *explanationes* oder *accessus ad poetas.*' Sporadic mention is found, mainly in M. Manitius, *Geschichte der lateinischen Literatur des Mittelalters* (München, 3 v. 1911–1931) especially I, 167; 482; 505; 512. III, 314; most of Manitius' references are to Schepss and Przychocki as below. L. Traube, *Vorlesungen und Abhandlungen* II, *Einleitung in die lateinische Philologie des Mittelalters* (ed. P. Lehmann, München 1911) 165: 'Man fasste diese sogennanten *accessus* öfters zusammen und hatte dann eine richtige Schulliteraturgeschichte. Es scheint, dass hierbei Remigius von Auxerre ein leitendes Beispiel war. Gewöhnlich sind die *accessus* nach bestimmten Gesichtspunkten angelegt. Man findet diese Gesichtspunkte der römischen Literatur zuerst bei Boethius. Da wird nach sechs Dingen gefragt: *intentio, utilitas, ordo, si germanus propriusque liber, inscriptio operis, ad quem philosophiae partem.* Später heisst es *in principio omnium librorum tria* [oder *quattuor* oder *quinque*] *requirenda esse videtur: persona, tempus, locus.*' P. Lehmann, 'Literaturgeschichte im Mittelalter I,' *Germanisch-romanische Monatschrift* 4 (1912) 572: '. . . Kommentaren älterer lateinischer Dichter vorangeschickt waren und kurz über den Autor und seine Schriften nach einem bestimmten Schema orientierten; in diesen *Accessus ad poetas,* die für die Einführung in die schulmässige Lektüre berechnet waren, hatte man literargeschichtliches Material.' G. Przychocki, 'Accessus Ovidiani ' [Symbolae ad veterum auctorum historiam atque ad medii aevi studia philologa], *Rosprawy Akademii Umiejetnosci Wydzial Filologizny* (*Dissertations of the Polish Academy of Sciences, Philological section*) Series III, 65–126 (Kraków 1911; also published separately, same year). G. Schepss, *Conradus Hirsaugiensis Dialogus super Auctores sive Didascalon* (Würzburg 1889). Karl Young, 'Chaucer's Appeal to the Platonic Deity,' *Speculum* 19 (1944) 1–13.

[2] Complete references to the studies made in these fields on the *accessus* will be given below when each of these fields will be explored as to its use.

1

evidence taken mainly from the confines of one particular field. In view of the fact that varying forms of the *accessus* appear to have been utilized in nearly all sections of the medieval school curriculum, such a viewpoint can hardly yield results that will give a comprehensive picture of the facts of the case.

It is undoubtedly true that the practice was very popular in the twelfth century as abundant evidence will show,[3] but it is also clear that there was a long tradition in the use of such an introduction in many branches and it seems probable that the fabric woven in the twelfth century drew its threads from many different sources in the preceding ages. The lines of growth of the tradition do not seem to have been independent. The ultimate source of the practice can perhaps be named with some degree of probability; it is to be hoped that further researches can unearth definitive evidence and give to the inventor a local habitation and a name. The course of development of certain of these items in commentators in several fields has not been without its influence on the growth of a particular science, by way of suggesting certain theoretical questions. Besides, from the whole discussion we are introduced to a technique of medieval teachers and students that will help to the ever-valuable end of enabling us to know more intimately the minds of our medieval forebears.

In the interest of clarity this discussion will treat of the work that has been done on this subject by scholars in their individual fields of medieval studies. At the end, the various points of contact and the many ramifications of the topic will be joined together in an attempt to give a clear picture of the history and development of the *accessus ad auctores*.

I. Historians of Medieval Latin Literature

The *locus classicus* for the discussion of this matter among literary historians has been Conrad of Hirschau, a Benedictine monk of the twelfth century. The work in question,[1] *Dialogus super auctores sive didascalon*, is a dialogue between *Magister* and *Discipulus* in which is explained the proper manner of entering upon the study of an *auctor*. After some preliminary remarks as to his purpose and point of view, the *Magister* briefly outlines the salient points as to the career and works of the *auctores* commonly studied in the classes of *Grammatica* in the twelfth century. The list of these *auctores* is of interest for the catholicity of Conrad's taste, and it is likely that his material is taken from the introductions to commentaries on the individual *auctores* or from codices containing collections of *accessus* without the commentaries on the text of the works. He treats of: Aesop, Avianus, Boethius, Cato, Cicero, Donatus, Homer, Juvenal, Lucan, Ovid, Persius, Prosper, Prudéntius, Sallust, Sedulius, Statius, Virgil and Theodulus.

---

[3] Cf. E. K. Rand, 'The Classics in the thirteenth century,' *Speculum* 4 (1929) 252.

[1] Cf. *supra*, p. 1 n. 1. 'Conradus Hirsaugiensis . . . natione Teutonicus, Spirensis dioecesis, vir in divinis scripturis et in saecularibus litteris valde peritus, philosophus, rhetor, musicus et poeta insignis, . . . multa praeclara composuit opuscula, in quibus ornata sententiarum dispositio et venusti sermonis cultura nulli veterum inferiorem suum declarat auctorem . . . Quidquid autem Conradus scripsit, Tullianam resonat eloquentiam . . . Claruit sub Conrado imperatore, a.d. 1140,' Fabricius III, 79, quoted by Schepss, *op. cit.* 8. As to Conrad, cf. M. Manitius, *op. cit.* III, 315.

Before treating of these individual *auctores* Conrad gives us the only theoretical discussion of the technique of the *accessus* that has come down to us from medieval times. From the following citation, it will be clear *a*) that he does not consider himself to be the inventor of the practice but is rather following a well-established tradition of the past; *b*) that this is a model for the treatment of all literary figures whether pagan or Christian, whether written in prose or verse; *c*) it was intended for very elementary students and did not pretend to be an exhaustive account of the *auctores*.

Discipulus: Saecularis disciplinae congrua meae tarditati dare spoponderas olim rudimenta, quibus a minoribus quibusdam auctoribus inciperem et per hos ad maiores pervenirem et gradus auctorum inferiorum occasio mihi fierent in discendo superiorum . . . *Magister*: Quid igitur in his dicendum ambagibus censes? Quid vel de quibus interrogas? *D*: Summatim et quodam breviario precor explicari a te, quid in singulis auctoribus scholasticis, quibus imbui floribunda tyrunculorum solent ingenia, requirendum sit idest qui auctor sit, quid, quantum, quando vel quomodo idest utrum metrice vel prosaice scripserit, qua etiam materia vel intentione opus cuiusque exordium sumpserit, ad quem finem ipsa scriptionum series relata sit . . . et si qua alia sunt sive in ecclesiasticis auctoribus seu gentilibus auctoribus requirenda. Quorum omnium brevis solutio videtur mihi quaedam ad auctores intellegendos magnos vel minimos introductio . . . Nec etiam a te magna requiro; quaero enim a te non ut totius domus apertae supellectilem scruteris, sed clausis claves adhibeas ostiis; non auctorum quaero lectionem vel expositionem, sed ex principio eorum idest materia vel intentione colligere medietatem et finem. *M*: Non autem erit difficile nobis inniti vestigiis aliorum et quasi ad portas introitum ad principia ducere, quorum noticiam quaeris auctorum . . . *Nec te lateat, quod in libris explanandis VII antiqui requirebant: auctorem, titulum operis, carminis qualitatem, scribentis intentionem, ordinem, numerum librorum, explanationem; sed moderni IIII requirenda censuerunt: operis materiam, scribentis intentionem, finalem causam et cui parti philosophiae subponatur quod scribitur.* *D*: Dic igitur, quid sit materia, quid intentio, quid causa finalis. *M*: Materia est unde constat quodlibet, unde et vocabulum trahit quasi mater rei; . . . Intentio est quid auctor intendat, quid, quantum, de quo scribere proponat. Porro finalis causa fructus legentis est; . . . de partibus autem philosophiae, quibus opus omne auctorum subponitur . . . Philosophia enim, licet simplex sit et uniformis in sui proprietate, dispertitur tamen in multa ratione disciplinae; dividitur igitur in tria, in logicam, phisicam, quibus VII artes quae liberales vocantur subponuntur, tercia ethica idest moralis, cui tractatus fere auctorum omnium innituntur, qui de moribus instituendis processisse probantur.[2]

Among the individual authors mentioned above, it will be useful to quote here what he chose to say about Boethius:

De Boetio quidem suis temporibus florentissimo nota est historia quomodo pro tuenda veritate a tiranno Theoderico carcerali squalore punitus sit, quot et quantos libros ante id tempus sive aliis transferendo vel exponendo seu dictando et alios ipse per se confecerit. Sed istum quem habemus in manibus in Consolationem sui et aliorum iniuste afflictorum ex persona miseri condolentis et philosophiae consolantis patet eum confecisse, quia post tantas vitae delicias hausto gustu doloris melius potuit ostendere miseriae qualitatem sibi prius ignotam, cuiuslibet dolentis et quodammodo de alto cadentis . . . *Materia* Boetii sunt philosophicae consolatrices sapientiae de quibus agit in hoc opere. *Intendit* autem iste quoslibet miseros in miseriis laborantes ex ipsa miseria retrahere et ad veri boni noticiam per mundi contemptum informare. *Utilitas* est ut ducti lege rationis prospera et adversa equaliter estimemus et ad veri boni ut beati esse possimus, appetitum festinemus . . . *Ethicae subponitur.* . . . *D*: Admiratione dignum videtur quod vir iste totus Catholicus

---

[2] *Dialogus* 20–33.

Fortunam tociens in hoc opere ponit et testimoniis divinis literam elegantem vacuam ostendit. *M*: Huius rei causa est et prima quidem quod qui inter hostes veritatis versabatur,
si testimoniis scripturae cingeret opus quod fecerat, incredulorum malicia combureret
quod non intellegebat; secunda causa est quod vir prudentissimus ad incertos temporalium
eventus demonstrandos ratione magis uti voluit quam scripturarum auctoritate, ut vel
sola ratione mundi contemptum persuaderet qui tunc temporis nihil ex auctoritate divina
ex perverso interprete vel lectore perficeret.[3]

It is clear, then, that the work of Conrad is a kind of compendium of literary
history such as an experienced and enterprising teacher would compile for the
convenience of his pupils at the outset of their studies. It has been suggested[4]
that the *Dialogus* is a link in the chain that began for Christian literature with
the *De viris illustribus* of St. Jerome, but the similarities between the two are
merely superficial —in that both wanted to give some information about the
life and work of a writer. There is no trace in St. Jerome's work of a stereotyped plan according to which all the *auctores* might be investigated. In the
work of Conrad, however, we have crystallized a definite school technique, a
handbook which would have been of great value to students, provided, of course,
they went on to the study of the texts themselves. It is to be hoped that the
Discipulus did not end his studies with some information about the *principium*,
neglecting altogether (and not merely for the moment) *medietatem et finem*!

The varying amounts of information on specific *auctores* and the diverse
points of view clearly betray the fact that Conrad is a compiler. The tendency
of mind thus manifested is an example of the preoccupation of the earlier Middle
Ages when men thought primarily of the need of preserving all that had been
handed down as to ancient times—the stream that began with Pliny was crystallized in St. Isidore of Seville in his *Etymologiae* and was carried on by the
Speculum of Vincent of Beauvais. In the field of theology, the *Florilegia*
point in the same direction. It might be somewhat surprising that collections of
accessus were not compiled earlier in the course of the Middle Ages, but the fact
that it was done in the twelfth century is but another indication of the increased
interest in classical *auctores* at that time.[5] These collections of introductions
to a large group of *auctores* may indicate that a more intensive reading of their
complete works made this type of thing necessary.

The first extended treatment of the *accessus* in modern times from the point
of view of literary history is to be found in the monograph of Przychocki whose
main interest lay in the fate of Ovid in the Middle Ages.[6] With a view to
illustrating what men of those times knew and thought of the personality,
career, and works of Ovid, he published for the first time some *accessus* to the
works of that poet, mainly from *Cod. Monacensis lat.* 19475. Having made use
of the *accessus* as a tool for his main purpose, Przychocki then turned to an anal-

---

[3] *Dialogus* 57–60.
[4] Schepss 10–11.
[5] Cf. C. H. Haskins, *The Renaissance of the Twelfth Century* (Cambridge, Mass. 1933)
93–126 and G. Paré, A. Brunet, P. Tremblay, *La Renaissance du XII*e *siècle* (Paris 1933)
56–179.
[6] Cf. *supra*, p. 1 n. 1.

ysis of the practice of the technique in the Middle Ages. As a preliminary to a review of his findings on that matter, a representative specimen of an *accessus* by a practitioner of *Grammatica* in the twelfth century may pardonably be quoted at some length here.[7]

Ovidii Epistularum: In principio huius libri VI sunt inquirenda: Vita poetae, titulus operis, intentio scribentis, materia, utilitas, cui parti philosophiae supponitur. Vita istius poetae talis est: Sulmonensis esse dicitur, quod ipse testatur: Sulmo mihi patria est. Ex Paeligno oppido autem natus patre Publio, matre vero Pelagia. Cuius frater Lucius ad rethoricam se contulit, iste vero in poetria studuit. Et sciendum est ante tempus Ovidii non esse factas epistolas Romae, sed Ovidius suo tempore ad imitationem cuiusdam Graeci fecit primas epistolas. *Titulus operis* sumitur a materia, quae sunt epistolae. Sumitur etiam a loco et a persona, ut Phormio et Eunuchus vel ab actu personarum, ut Auctontumerumenos [sic], id est: se ipsum excrucians, et sic faciunt astra vel a materia, ut Tullius de amicitia. Iste quoque a materia sumitur, intitulatur enim a quibusdam 'Ovidii epistolarum' propter hanc causam, quia diversae sunt epistolae in hoc volumine, quae poterant mitti vel mittebantur Graecis viris in obsidione Troiae manentibus, vel illuc tendentibus, aut inde redeuntibus cuique de uxore sua. 'Epi': Graece, Latine: supra; 'stola': missa. Litterae mittuntur propter necessariam causam aliquam et sumuntur a personis, quae sunt eius materia. Unde quidem intitulant eum 'Ovidium heroum', id est matronarum, vel 'Liber heroidos'. 'Heros, herois' Graece est masculinum et significat Graecas mulieres nobiles. Ideo autem sic intitulatus est, quia scriptus est sub personis illarum Graecarum nobilium mulierum, quarum viri demorabantur in obsidione Troiae et quia Heroides excellentiores matronae erant in Graecia, a quibus et maxima parte amatoribus suis hae epistolae mittebantur.

Hoc de titulo, nunc de intentione videamus. *Intentio* eius est de triplici genere amoris, stulti, incesti, furiosi scribere. De stulto habet exemplum per Phyllidem, quae Demophoonti reditum, ut suis disponeret concessit; quae expectare non valens, ex amoris intemperantia se laqueo suspendit. Incesti habet exemplum per Helenam quae Paridi nupsit, legitimo viro suo sumpta Menelao. Furiosi habet exemplum per Canacen, quae Machareum fratrem suum dilexit. *Aliter: Intentio huius libri* est commendare castum amorem sub specie quarundam Heroidum id est nobilium Graecarum mulierum, quarum una erat uxor Penelopes Ulixis vel vituperare incestum amorem sub specie incestarum matronarum, quarum una fuit Phaedra. *Aliter*: intentio sua est quasdam ex illis committentibus epistolas laudare de castitate sua, quasdam autem reprehendere de incesto amore. *Aliter*: Intentio sua est, cum in praeceptis de arte amatoria non ostendit, quo modo aliquis per epistolas sollicitaretur, illud his exsequitur. *Aliter*: Intentio sua est in hoc libro hortari ad virtutes et redarguere vitia. Ipse accusatus fuit apud Caesarem, quia scriptis suis Romanas matronas illicitos amores docuisset. Unde librum scripsit eis, istud exemplum proponens, ut sciant, amando quas debeant imitari, quas non. Sciendum quoque est, quod cum in toto libro hanc et supradictas habeat intentiones, praeterea duas habet in hoc libro, unam generalem, et aliam specialem. Generalem delectari et communiter prodesse. Specialem habet intentionem sicut in singulis epistulis, aut laudando castum amorem, ut in hoc: Hanc tua Penelope . . . aut vituperando incestum amorem, ut in illa: Quam nisi tu dederis . . . Et bene diversae epistolae diversas intentiones habent

---

[7] *Monac. lat.* 19475 (olim *Tegernseensis* 1475, s. xii) is a collection of *accessus* to the following *auctores*: Ovid (*Epp.*), Prudentius, Cato, Avianus, Maximianus, Homerus Latinus, Physiologus, Theodulus, Arator, Prosper, Sedulius, Ovid (*Ars Amat.*, *Remedia*, *Ex Ponto*, *Tristia*, *Amores*, *Fasti*), Lucan, Cicero, Boethius, Priscian, Horace. MSS catalogues often suggest and occasionally mention the presence of *accessus*; cf. *Vat. lat.* 1593 (Ovid, *Metamorph.*) s. xii ex. (*Codices Vaticani Latini*, ed. B. Nogara, Romae 1912, I, 87); *Vat. Reg.* 72, 138, 230 (*Codices Reginenses Latini in Bibliotheca Vaticana*, ed. A. Wilmart, Romae 1937). For references to other MSS, cf. Przychocki 79.

quia dum quasdam de castitate commendare alias de incesto amore reprehendere proposuit, diversa intendebat. *Materia sua* sunt epistolae suae sive eas scribentes, scilicet maritatae. *Utilitas vel finalis causa* secundum intentiones diversificatur, vel illicitorum vel stultorum amorum cognitio vel quo modo per effectum ipsius castitatis commodum consequamur. Vel finalis causa est, ut per commendationem caste amantium ad castos amores nos invitet, vel ut visa utilitate, quae ex legitimo amore procedit visisque infortuniis vel incommoditatibus, quae ex illicito et stulto amore proveniunt et stultum et illicitum repellamus et fugiamus et legitimo adhaereamus. *Ethicae supponitur*, quia de iusto amore instruit. . . .[8]

The anonymous author's main interest, as is evident, lay in the moral aspects of the work of Ovid. By far the largest share of his remarks are on that topic and the various *intentiones* given would seem to indicate vacillation on his part, until it becomes clear that he is attempting to explain the *intentiones speciales* of Ovid in the different poems of the collection. The elementary nature of his remarks[9] in general gives the impression that he is trying to adapt to his subject a school technique that he had inherited. Many examples of *accessus* can be seen that strike a much higher level of learning and which would give to a beginner a much clearer orientation in his studies.

Przychocki's analysis of this and other specimens of *accessus* begins with some suggestions as to the origin of two of the items, namely, *utilitas* and *cui parti philosophiae supponatur*. In these he finds to his satisfaction the baneful influence of scholastic philosophy and the apparently scarcely less regrettable interest of the medieval teacher in the Christian religion.

Sic itaque *utilitas* et quaestio *cui parti philosophiae opus supponatur* aperte suos produnt fontes . . . *christianam* intellege *doctrinam* et quae eius addicta et dedita fuit ancilla *scholasticam philosophiam*. De philosophia res ex se intellegitur, *cum nemo ignoret quae medio aevo 'philosophiae' fuerint studia*, ad utilitatis vero vim et originem accuratius exponendam etiam haec, quae in Conrado . . . velim conferas . . . 'utilitatem quae est veritatis cognitio et rectae fidei confirmatio in lectore versari manifestum est.'[10]

It is regrettable that these caustic remarks could not have been reserved for a topic which deserved them better, especially in view of the fact that it is certain that the two items, *utilitas* and *cui parti philosophiae* have nothing whatever to do with scholastic philosophy as they are found in *accessus* long before the most enthusiastic medievalist would place the date of the beginning of scholasticism. Further, the question of both topics was raised by pagans, some of whom were known for their opposition to Christianity. This error, however, of Przychocki is excusable since he apparently had no idea of the widespread use of this technique in the early centuries of our era.[11]

[8] Przychocki, *op. cit.* 80–85.

[9] Cf. Conrad, *supra*, p. 3: 'Quorum omnium brevis solutio videtur mihi quaedam ad auctores intelligendos . . . introductio. . . . Nec etiam a te magna requiro; . . . non ut totius domus apertae supellectilem scruteris, sed clausis claves adhibeas ostiis; non auctorum quaero lectionem vel explicationem. . . .'

[10] Conrad, *Dialogus* 45; Przychocki, *op. cit.* 106; the sections of the text italicized above are, in Przychocki, in roman but with a space between the letters to make them stand out.

[11] The proofs of these statements will be given *in extenso* in the later chapters of this paper when we treat of the rhetoricians and dialecticians.

The stress which the writer of the *accessus* quoted above placed on *utilitas* and *cui parti philosophiae supponatur* further provoked Przychocki because this forced the medieval commentator into apparently ridiculous statements as to the *intentio* of Ovid in the *Heroides*.

Nimirum elegiae illae maxima utilitate repletae esse videbantur, *ethicae supponitur, quia de moribus tractent*, cum egregii isti magistri atque doctores *scholasticae*, quae dicitur *philosophiae somniis decepti atque christianae doctrinae modum excedentes*, in eiusmodi carminibus lasciva vitia ista in auctoribus nequiquam delectandi studio sed quasi ignominiae nota iniusta reprehendendi voluntate prolata esse crederent. Et praecipue discrimine illo, quod inter auctoris intercedat et personae loquentis intentionem, perperam invento mirum in modum pullulat ac luxuriat eorum insipientia. Nam hoc modo, e.g. de Ovidiana Paridis epistola disputant: 'Cuius intentio duplex est, scilicet scribentis et, Helenam ad suum amorem detrahere et eam exhortari ut ipsum diligat. Intentio auctoris est, Paridem de proditione et illicito amore reprehendere sq.' At mehercule, quonam docti oraculo hanc piam Ovidii eruerunt intentionem, de qua, inter sanos quidem, nihil constat?[12]

The heavy-handed irony of this passage, and especially the phrase 'mirum in modum pullulat et luxuriat eorum insipientia', is interesting as an example of that curious attitude of scholars who devote themselves to the study of the Middle Ages only to take obvious delight in ridiculing the stupidity of medieval authors. Przychocki is also annoyed at this point in his analysis because of a long section in Conrad's treatment of Ovid where he warns his students against the danger of moral contagion from reading works such as those of Ovid, which are lacking in moral sense. If I understand this curiously obscure

---

[12] Przychocki 103. Apparently Przychocki got his notion of the influence of scholastic philosophy on the development of the *accessus* from the remarks of R. Ehwald, 'Ad historiam carminum ovidianorum recensionemque symbolae,' *Programm des Herzoglichen Gymnasium Ernestinum zu Gotha* 2 (1892) 1–2, from which he quotes in another connection: 'Nolo fusius nunc in haec ipsa inquirere eorumque initia, quae tamen omnia cum Aristotelicae philosophiae studiis coniuncta ad unum quasi fontem referenda esse clamat codicum diversissimorum consensus, nec tertio decimo demum saeculo scholasticum hunc excultum esse usum, sed prioribus iam saeculis in monasteriorum scholis illa ratione scriptores veteres esse explicatos saeculi undecimi docet Benedictoburanus . . . commentarium metamorphoseon cum praefatione continens in quo leguntur haecce, ex quibus etiam ante scriptores ipsius aetatis latiore quasi circuitu eadem adnotari solita esse concludas: cum multa possent inquiri in capite uniuscuiusque libri, moderni autem gaudentes brevitate tria . . . principaliter inquirenda statuere id est materiam intentionem et cui parti philosophiae supponatur.' Ehwald in this connection refers to F. Haase, *De medii aevi studiis philologicis* (Breslau 1856) 13: 'Non autem credendum est fuisse magnum quoddam studium historiae litterariae, quo qui vera nesciebant, falsa effingere adducerentur; a quo studio quantopere abhorruerint medii aevi docti homines, saepissime ii testati sunt qui post vulgatam philosophiam Aristotelicam commentarios in libros cuiuslibet generis scripserunt; hi enim praefatione constanter sic composita usi, ut libri de quo agerent quattuor causas explicarent, ubi causam efficientem memorabant, brevissime plerumque libri auctorem appellabant, raro aliqua de eius vita et scriptis addebant.' Both of these inferences are drawn from the late (13th-century) use of the *accessus*; cf. Paré–Brunet–Tremblay, *op. cit.* 116, 'Ces introductions, dont le plan consiste régulièrement . . . à exposer les causes efficiente, matérielle, formelle et finale de l'ouvrage, telles qu'on en rencontre souvent au xiiie siècle.' They do not seem to refer to the invention of the technique in the works of early Aristotelian commentators, a conclusion which, as we shall see, can be maintained.

passage aright, it appears that Przychocki is in one breath objecting to finding some good intentions in Ovid, and in the next, condemning the author for recognizing amorality when he meets it.   However, such recriminations are of little value in finding the source of the medieval use of the *accessus*, and can well be dismissed.

What is of importance, however, for an understanding of the mind of the Middle Ages, is this whole question of reading *intentiones* into the mind of Ovid and other ancient authors.   Nothing that we know of Ovid would lead us to suspect that morality and its promotion was one of the aims of his literary life.   Yet, medieval authors are continually talking as if his motive was as high and his intention as spiritual as that of any of the Fathers in their satires on the immoralities of their times.   This subject is most important for our understanding of our medieval forebears and hence we may be pardoned for what might seem to be a rather long digression.   The remarkable *Fortleben* of Ovid in the Middle Ages is well known.[13]   Popular tradition had, on one side, made of him a teacher of morals, a Christian preacher, and they even 'found' a form of *retractatio* in which, having seen the light of Faith, Ovid changed the opening lines of the Metamorphoses so that it began with an invocation of the Holy Trinity.   The high point of this half of the tradition was crystallized in a preface to the spurious *De vetula*, supposed to have been found in his tomb in Pontus: 'Ad ultimum ponit fidem suam tractans egregissime de incarnatione

---

[13] A detailed discussion of this matter would go far beyond the scope of this paper, but out of the welter of bibliographical data that is given on the subject, the following are really valuable.   H. Bartsch, *Albrecht von Halberstadt und Ovid im Mittelalter* (Quedlinburg 1861) is the source of much else that has been written along these lines; D. Comparetti, *Virgil in the Middle Ages* (New York 1929) is mainly on Virgil but has many remarks on Ovid; F. Peeters, *Les Fastes d'Ovide* (Bruxelles 1938); G. Schevill, *Ovid and the Renaissance in Spain* (Berkeley 1916) in which the first chapter gives a survey of the data outside of Spain; J. Sedlmayer, 'Beiträge zur Geschichte der Ovidienstudien im Mittelalter,' *Wiener Studien* 6 (1884); B. Nogara, 'Di alcune vite e commenti medioevali di Ovidio,' *Miscellanea Ceriani* (Milano 1910) is most informative and suggestive; G. Pansa, *Ovidio nel medioevo e nella tradizione popolare* (Sulmona 1924) and A. De Nino, *Ovidio nella tradizione popolare di Sulmona* (Casalbordino 1886) contain many oral traditions which provide a contrast to the literary traditions.   F. Ghislaberti, *Integumenta Ovidii Joannis de Garlandia* (Milano 1933); L. J. Paetow, *The Battle of the Seven Liberal Arts* (Berkeley 1929) and *The Arts Course in Mediaeval Universities* (Berkeley 1914); G. Paris, *Les anciennes versions françaises de l'Art d'aimer et des Remèdes d'Amour d'Ovide* (Paris 1884) is essential for the study of Ovid's influence on French literature; the following will be helpful: E. Faral, *Recherches sur les sources latines des contes et romans courtois du moyen-âge* (Paris 1913); A. Jeanroy, *Les origines de la poésie lyrique en France au moyen âge* (Paris 1925); a good summary will be found in E. K. Rand, *Ovid and His Influence* (Debt to Greece and Rome, Boston 1924) and the same author's 'The Metamorphoses of Ovid in *Le Roman de la Rose*,' *Studies in the History of Culture* (1942) is a detailed study of the influence of Ovid on Jean de Meun.   On MSS of Ovid cf. M. Manitius, 'Beiträge zur Geschichte römischer Dichter im Mittelalter,' *Philologus* 47 (1889) and 'Philologisches aus alten Bibliothekskatalogen,' *Rheinisches Museum* (1892); also H. Buttenweiser, 'Manuscripts of Ovid's *Fasti*: The Ovidian Tradition in the Middle Ages,' *Trans. Amer. Philol. Assoc.* 71 (1940) 45–51.   For Chaucer cf. E. F. Shannon, *Chaucer and the Roman Poets* (Harvard Studies in Comp. Lit. 7, Cambridge, Mass. 1929).

ihesu christi, et de passione, de resurrectione et de ascensione et de vita beate marie virginis et de assumptione in celum.'[14]

On the other hand, a second stream of the tradition portrayed Ovid as a magician, in league with the devil and lost forever in hell. It is the former, that of Ovid the Good, in which we are interested at the moment. Very often in medieval writers on Ovid, one would get the impression that they thoroughly believed the legends that made him a Saint and a teacher of morals, and in this connection there are several strong currents in medieval thought that must be taken into consideration.

1. *The Practice of Allegory.* By no means a Christian invention, the allegorical interpretation of Homer was suggested by Theagenes of Rhegium in the sixth century B.C.[15] Great strides were made in its use by Philo Judaeus, who sought to show that there was nothing in the Septuagint that conflicted with Platonism. Clement of Alexandria and Origen were the heirs of this tradition and the latter held that the whole of Scripture had a spiritual meaning, although not always a literal sense.[16] His explanation of the *sensus allegoricus*, *moralis*, and *anagogicus* was one of the many sources of his influence on the Fathers. St. Jerome, St. Augustine, St. Ambrose, and especially St. Gregory the Great felt a tremendous fascination for this method, and through *florilegia* the practice grew apace throughout the Middle Ages in the work of scriptural exegetes, and would have been completely familiar to any cleric of the times.

2. *Spoliatio Aegyptiorum.* This theme, probably introduced by St. Augustine, was the most important influence in giving a *rationale* to the study of pagan literature by Christians. St. Jerome's famous Dream and St. Augustine's regrets of his youthful weeping over the woes of Dido are but two of many examples of the struggle undergone by the early Christians when faced with the problem of exposing the young to the allurements of pagan antiquity. The

---

[14] *Vat. lat.* 1479; cf. B. Nogara, *Miscellanea Ceriani* (*supra*, p. 8 n. 13).

[15] J. E. Sandys, *A History of Classical Scholarship*, 3 vols. (Cambridge 1906) I, 29.

[16] Origen, *De Principiis* IV, 11 (GCS, *Origines Werke* V, ed. P. Koetschau, Leipzig 1913, pp. 311–312): 'Tripliciter ergo describere oportet in anima sua unumquemque divinarum intelligentiam litterarum: id est ut simpliciores quique aedificentur ab ipso, ut ita dixerim, corpore scripturarum (sic enim appellamus communem illum et historialem intellectum); si qui vero aliquantum iam proficere coeperunt et possunt amplius aliquid intueri, ab ipsa scripturae anima aedificentur; qui vero perfecti sunt et similes his, de quibus apostolus dicit: "Sapientiam autem loquimur inter perfectos, sapientiam vero non huius saeculi neque principum huius saeculi, qui destruentur, sed loquimur dei sapientiam in mysterio absconditam, quam praedestinavit deus ante saecula in gloriam nostram," hi tales ab ipsa "spiritali lege," "quae umbram habet futurorum bonorum," tamquam ab spiritu aedificentur. Sicut ergo homo constare dicitur ex corpore et anima et spiritu, ita etiam sancta scriptura, quae ad hominum salutem divina largitione concessa est.' Noteworthy also is Gregorius Magnus, *Hom. xv in Evangelia* (PL 76, 1131) where he is explaining Luke viii, 4–15. It is the parable of the seed that fell by the wayside, among thorns, on rocks and on good ground, which was explained by Christ to the Apostles as the word of God. Gregory remarks: 'Unde et idem Dominus per semetipsum dignatus est exponere quod dicebat, *ut sciatis rerum significationes quaerere in iis quae per semetipsum noluit explanare.* Exponendo ergo quod dixit figurate se loqui innotuit, quatenus certos vos redderet cum vobis nostra fragilitas verborum illius figuras aperiret.'

universal acceptance of the *De doctrina christiana* in the Middle Ages would have made this passage the *locus classicus*.[17]

Sicut enim Aegyptii non solum idola habebant et onera gravia quae populus Israel detestaretur et fugeret sed etiam vasa atque ornamenta de auro et argento et vestem, quae ille populus exiens de Aegypto, sibi potius tamquam ad usum meliorem clanculo vindicavit; non auctoritate propria, sed praecepto Dei, ipsis Aegyptiis nescienter commodantibus ea quibus non bene utebantur; *sic doctrinae omnes Gentilium non solum simulata et superstitiosa figmenta gravesque sarcinas supervacanei laboris habent quae unusquisque nostrum, duce Christo, de societate Gentilium exiens, debet abominari atque devitare, sed etiam liberales disciplinas usui veritatis aptiores, et quaedam morum praecepta utilissima continent, deque ipso uno Deo colendo nonnulla vere inveniuntur apud eos; quod eorum tamquam aurum et argentum, quod non ipsi instituerunt sed de quibusdam quasi metallis divinae providentiae, quae ubique infusa est, eruerunt, et quo perverse atque iniuriose ad obsequia daemonum abutuntur, cum ab eorum misera societate sese animo separat, debet ab eis auferre Christianus ad usum iustum praedicandi evangelii.*[18]

Under the impulse of this rationalization, Christian writers would feel that they were only utilizing their own heritage, God's truth, when they found it in pagan literature and they could adapt it to any use they might please.

3. *Captiva Gentilis.* Allied to the preceding theme is the one taken from the prescription of Jewish Law as given in Deuteronomy,[19] whereby the hair must be clipped and the nails pared, of a gentile captive woman, if she were to become the wife of a Jew. Its application to the matter of pagan literature we have in the words of Rhabanus Maurus:

Poemata autem et libros gentilium si velimus propter flores eloquentiae legere, typus mulieris captivi tenendus est, quam Deuteronomium describit et Dominum ita praecepisse commemorat, ut si Israelites eam habere vellet uxorem, calvitium ei faciet, ungues praesecet, pilos auferat, et cum munda fuerit effecta, tunc transeat in uxoris amplexus. Haec si secundum literam intelligimus, nonne ridicula sunt? Itaque et nos facere solemus, hocque facere debemus quando poetas gentiles legimus, quando in manus nostras libri veniunt sapientiae saecularis, si quid in eis utile reperimus, ad nostrum dogma convertimus; si quid vero superfluum de idolis, de amore, de cura saecularium rerum, haec radamus, his calvitium inducamus, haec in unguium more ferro acutissimo desecemus. Hoc tamen prae omnibus cavere debemus, ne haec licentia nostra offendiculum fiat infirmis; ne pereat qui infirmus est in scientia nostra frater, propter quem Christus mortuus est, si viderit in idolio nos recumbentes.[20]

In accordance with this principle a judicious process of selection would have been in order. In the case of the *Heroides*, it would be very easy to adapt to Christian use (*ad nostrum dogma convertere*) the letter of Penelope to Ulysses, and of Laodamia to Protesilaos, in which there is nothing morally objectionable.

[17] St. Jerome, *Ep.* xxii, 30 *Ad Eustochium*, (ed. I. Hilberg, CSEL 54, 1910) 189 and St. Augustine, *Confessiones* I, xiii (ed. P. Knöll, Leipzig 1926) 15.

[18] St. Augustine, *De doctrina christiana* II, 60 (Florilegium Patristicum 24, ed. H. J. Vogels, Bonn 1930) 46. Cf. Exod. iii, 22; xi, 2; xii, 35; also Origen, PG 11, 1077, 1088 (Koetschau, fasc. IV).

[19] Deut. xxi, 10–13: Si egressus fueris ad pugnam contra inimicos tuos, et tradiderit eos Dominus Deus tuus in manu tua, captivosque duxeris, et videris in numerum captivorum. mulierem pulchram, et adamaveris eam, voluerisque habere uxorem, introduces eam in domum tuam; quae radet caesariem et circumcidet ungues et deponet vestem in qua capta est.'

[20] Rhabanus Maurus, *De clericorum institutione* III, 18 (PL 107, 396); cf. St. Jerome, *Ep.* lxx, 2, 5.

4. *Auctores authentici.* The writers of antiquity, both pagan and Christian, were in the medieval schools known as *auctores*, writers who possessed an *auctoritas* to which respect and admiration were due. The 'canon' of *auctores* rigorously excluded contemporary writers who were merely *lectores*. This *auctoritas* had to be maintained and it was often done in what might appear to be rather singular fashion. The *auctor* was cited but his words were interpreted to suit the purpose of the writer. This attempt to maintain the *auctoritas* of the revered figure of the past, even when twisting his words into an opposite meaning, is a sure index of the admiration in which he was held. Rather than contradict or condemn an *auctor*, the writer was content to interpret. *Exponere reverenter*, or simply *exponere*, became the customary process of face-saving for the *auctor*. Thus he often became merely the occasion taken by a writer to teach some principle that he had to heart.[21]

> En expliquant leur texte, les glossateurs ne cherchent pas à entendre la pensée de leur auteur, mais à enseigner la science elle-même que l'on supposait y être contenue. Un auteur authentique, comme on disait alors, ne peut ni se tromper, ni se contredire, ni suivre un plan défectueux, ni être en désaccord avec un autre auteur authentique. On avait recours aux artifices de l'exégèse les plus forcés pour accomoder la lettre du texte à ce que l'on considérait comme la vérité.[22]

When we remember that such lists of *auctores* might find Virgil, Ovid, Prudentius, Sedulius, Statius, Juvenal, Arator, and Horace cheek by jowl, we can see that all of them would be considered to be equally in possession of the truth by virtue of being *auctores*, and hence they must be made to speak with one voice. Perhaps in such a treatment of an *auctor*, the original views of the pagan writer might be rather hastily baptized, but in view of the supposition of the above points, viz., that all truth was from God and that what the gentiles had possessed in obscure and shadowy fashion should be illumined by the eye of Faith, a medieval writer would merely consider that he was filling out the picture as his *auctoritas* would have done if only he had had the opportunity. Everything was grist for the mill of the Christian writer, since he felt that all truth, implicit and explicit, was his for the taking. Far from childish naïveté is this independence of mind and command over his material. The aim was eminently practical and the writer got from his ancient source a glimmering of the truth that it was his object to teach. In view of the many condemnations of pagan immorality of which we have evidence, it is impossible to suppose that the medieval writer really believed that Ovid, for instance, had a high moral purpose in writing the *Ars amatoria*. Ovid, as an *auctor*, was the possession of the teacher of the Middle Ages and he could be used for whatever purpose the teacher wished. Anything in Ovid that was in accord with revealed truth, was God's truth from the beginning; anything that contradicted it, had to be interpreted in a way that would save, externally, the *auctor*, and that could

[21] Cf. Paré–Brunet–Tremblay, *op. cit.* 147–149.

[22] C. Thurot, 'Extraits de divers manuscrits latins pour servir à l'histoire des doctrines grammaticales au moyen âge,' *Notices et extraits des manuscrits de la Bibliothèque Nationale* 22, 2 (1868) 103–104.

be used for the instruction of his pupils. The medieval teacher would doubtless be amused at our suspicions of his intelligence.[23]

Continuing his analysis of the *accessus*, Przychocki quotes the opening lines of Servius' commentary on the Aeneid: 'In exponendis auctoribus haec consideranda sunt: poetae vita, titulus operis, qualitas carminis, scribentis intentio, numerus librorum, ordo librorum, explanatio.'[24] This he believes to be the source by which the *accessus* came to the twelfth century and as clinching proof of this, he quotes from a fifteenth century manuscript on the Metamorphoses of Ovid: 'Quoniam ut ait Servius super Aeneida, in exponendis auctoribus haec consideranda sunt . . . etc.'[25] He then quotes Conrad of Hirschau referring to the difference of practice in his times and in the past: 'Nec te lateat quod VII antiqui requirebant . . .' and finally concludes with these words: 'Antiquorum appellationem his quidem ad Vergilii Servianos commentarios referre iam non est cur dubitemus . . .'[26] Granting for the sake of the discussion that Conrad might have meant Servius when he spoke of *antiqui*, there is still considerable reason for doubt that this settles the whole question as to the provenience of the *accessus* in the twelfth century. It is true that Conrad has the same items in his enumeration that Servius has, but Servius was well known in the Middle Ages, and the fact that a fifteenth-century writer said that he found it in Servius is not quite sufficient proof that it came into Latin scholarship through Servius. The question is considerably more complicated than Przychocki suspected. The vagueness of his conclusion apparently became clear to him, as he goes on to adduce further evidence, a commentary on Sedulius of the twelfth century, which makes use of a somewhat different version: 'Possumus hic considerare: Quis, quid, cur, quando, ubi [quo modo], quibus facultatibus, i.e. tempus, locus et persona, res causa, qualitas, facultas.'[27]

[23] Distinctly refreshing is the viewpoint of Douglas Bush, *Mythology and the Renaissance Tradition* (Minneapolis 1932) 6, 12: '. . . the genial Ovid would probably have been less disturbed than [modern] scholars if he had known not merely that he would not wholly die, but that through the centuries he would be, like Caesar's wife, all things to all men. . . . Some, though by no means all of the elements of that popularity [of Ovid in the Middle Ages] were alien to the real Ovid, but we can ill afford to patronize medieval students who, whatever their occasional vagaries, had a vital contact with Latin literature. Their classical past was a usable one—as ours hardly is—and the diversity of uses that the Latin authors served is the best proof of a fruitful tradition. . . . How was a medieval translator to . . . make intelligible to readers such a poem as the Ars Amatoria? With the self-confidence and independence that is sometimes called medieval naïveté he made over Ovid for his own purposes and to suit his own world.' When a humane openmindedness such as this becomes the caracteristic trait of writers on the Middle Ages we shall no longer have discussions to which the word of Abailard—said, no doubt unfairly, of Anselm of Laon—applies: 'Cum ignem accenderet, domum suam fumo implebat, non luce illustrabat' (PL 178, 123).

[24] Przychocki, *op. cit.* 108. Thilo–Hagen, *Servii Grammatici in Vergilii Aeneidos* (Leipzig 1923) I, 1–3. Cf. *Vita Vergilii Donatiana*, in J. Brummer, *Vitae Vergilianae* (Leipzig 1912) 11–19.

[25] *Vat. lat.* 2781; Przychocki 108.

[26] Przychocki 110.

[27] *Cod. Marcianus*, s. xii.

He then shows the superficial equivalence of these terms of the common-place of rhetorical studies—the possible circumstances in which an incident took place—and he implies that this is the source of the normal version of the *accessus*. As proof of this, he cites once again the words of Conrad: 'Summatim et quodam breviario . . .' and by a most curious oversight omits, without any indication of a gap in the quotation, the italicized words: 'requirendum sit idest *qui auctor sit, quid, quantum, quando vel quomodo idest*, utrum metrice . . .' which would have strengthened his case for the connection between the two forms of the *accessus*.[28] Still, on the other hand, the fact that Conrad separates these two forms in his discussion, might seem to imply that the normal form (which is the one used in his subsequent discussion of individual authors) was the traditional one. These *circumstantiae* Przychocki also finds in other Latin manuscripts and in *Monac.* 18058, in which they are given in Greek. He further adduces the pseudo-Augustinus, *De rhetorica*, and Fortunatianus, *Ars rhetorica*.[29] Going back to Greek rhetoricians, he quotes from Theon, Hermogenes, and Aphthonius several passages in which they are discussing Narration and the formation of the argument, for which they prescribe the use of the *circumstantiae*. The passage from Hermogenes follows:[30]

περίστασις δέ ἐστι τὸ πᾶν ἐν ἡμῖν καὶ λόγοις καὶ πράγμασι καὶ δίκαις καὶ ὑποθέσεσι καὶ βίῳ, τόπος, χρόνος, τρόπος, πρόσωπον, αἰτία, πρᾶγμα. Προστιθέασι δὲ οἱ φιλόσοφοι καὶ ἕβδομόν τι, τὴν ὕλην. . . .

This and the passages from Theon and Aphthonius will be discussed later when we come to the use of the *accessus* by the followers of these rhetoricians. Przychocki then concludes his analysis thus:

Quae cum adeo sint manifesta, iam nemo erit certe, quin videat Graecos fuisse, qui illi priori (quod ad Servium rettulimus) et huic alteri (quod postremo loco examinavimus) accessuum generi communem praebuissent fontem; hi ambo autem exeuntis iam antiquitatis Latini auctores, Augustinum intellege et Fortunatianum (Aphthonii fere aequales), viam monstrant, qua doctrina illa, a Graecis rhetoricae artis scriptoribus exculta, recentiorum rhetorum latinorum libris interpositis in medii aevi Occidentis scholas pervenerit, ubi ad auctores interpretandos praecipue esset adhibita. Hic autem omnibus huius aetatis temporibus, quod quidem diversissimorum exemplorum docet consensus, usurpata, adeo percrebuit, ut normae prorsus et praescripti vim aut quasi κανόνος, quem Graeci dicunt, auctoritatem sit adepta. . . . Accessus erant omnium qui sibi auctores interpretandos proposuissent, communis, ut ita dicam, provincia, omnes sine nomine vulgati tantum apparent.[31]

---

[28] Cf. *supra*, p. 3.

[29] C. Halm, *Rhetores minores latini* (Leipzig 1863) I, 141; I, 102–103. To these may be added C. Julius Victor, *Ars rhetorica* (Halm 374, 424) and Albinus, *De arte rhetorica dialogus* (*ibid.* 527): 'Plenaria causa septem habet circumstantias, personam, factum, tempus, locum, modum, occasionem, facultatem. In persona quaeritur quis fecerit, in facto quid fecerit, in tempore quando fecerit, in loco ubi factum sit, in modo quomodo fieri potuisset, in occasione cur facere voluisset, in facultate, si ei suppeditaret potestas faciendi.'

[30] H. Rabe, *Rhetores graeci* VI (Leipzig 1913) 140.

[31] Przychocki 114–115.

We may take it then that, according to Przychocki, the ultimate source of
the *accessus* lies in the rhetorical use of *circumstantiae*, which later writers
adapted until it took the form we know of the *accessus*. This conclusion would
seem to be open to serious doubt in the light of the findings of the present in-
vestigation. Later Greek rhetoricians, it is true, have the developed form of the
accessus, but it seems probable that they got it from the philosophers. The
source is undoubtedly Greek, but it does not seem possible to trace, with certainty, the origin of the practice to its first inventor. It is hoped that the rest
of this discussion will supplement and clarify many of the points which in the
monograph of Przychocki suffered from narrowness of viewpoint.

II. The Accessus among the Lawyers

a) *Roman Law*

The flourishing rebirth of the study of the literary *auctores*, mainly in France,
in the twelfth century, was paralleled in Bologna with the rise there, of the
schools of law.[1] The beginnings of the law school at Bologna are shrouded in
legend and it appears that the facts have tended to become overlaid with a
veneer of patriotism, aided by a perfervid imagination. The story is told that
the Justinian Digest came to light again, after centuries of oblivion, as spoils
of a raid made on Amalfi, by a band of Pisan marauders, in 1136.[2] It is certain,

---

[1] Roman law as codified by Justinian was in the Middle Ages known as the *Corpus iuris
civilis*, and Digest, Code, Institutes, and Novels were grouped, somewhat arbitrarily, into
a) three *Digesta* (*Digestum Vetus, Infortiatum, Digestum Novum*), b) the *Codex* [I–IX],
c) the *Tres Libri* [*Cod.* X–XII], d) the *Instituta*, e) the *Authenticum* (Novellae). Cf. H.
D. Hazeltine, 'Roman and Canon Law in the Middle Ages,' CMH V, 697–764; F. C. von
Savigny, *Geschichte des römischen Rechts im Mittelalter*, III (2nd ed. Heidelberg 1834)
422–504.

[2] The sources for this story are given by Savigny, *Geschichte* III, 92–102 and are mainly:
an Italian chronicle of the fourteenth century which says: 'E per commandamento de
esso sommo Pontefice Papa Innocenzio II li pisani pridie nonas augusti armorno 46 galee:
furono alla costa de Malfi et quello di per forza lo preseno cum septe galee e doe naue: in
la quale citta trouorno le pandette composte dalla Cesarea Majesta de Justiniano Imperatore; dopoi brusunno quella, e l'altro di andorno a trani; et quello preseno per forza.'
The second item is to be found in an historical poem of the fourteenth century, reading:

> Malfia Parthenopes datur et quando omne per aequor
> Unde fuit liber Pisanis gestus ab illis
> Juris, et est Pisis Pandecta Caesaris alti.

Savigny rejects the story, leaning on the testimony of Odofredus who mentions that a copy
of the Digest had been brought to Pisa from Constantinople in the time of Justinian. He
concludes: 'Und so ist also die ganze Sache noch immer unter die zahlreichen Fabeln zu
rechnen, wodurch der Patriotismus der Italiener die Ehre der Vaterstadt zu verherrlichen
suchte.' To this negative testimony may be added the account in a twelfth-century
chronicle written by a contemporary: 'A. D. MCXXXVI. Pridie nonas Augusti fuerunt
Pisani cum xliv galeis super Malfim et ipso die capta est, et cum septem galeis et duabus
aliis multis navibus, combusta est et prorsus exspoliata est. Eadem vero die Trani capta
est.' This chronicle continues with other events and makes no mention of the finding of
the Pandects. The similarity between this and the Italian account given above suggests
that the contemporary record was embellished two centuries later. Cf. *Annales Pisani di
Bernardo Maragone*, in Muratori, *Rer. Ital. Scriptores* VI, ii, 9–10 (ed. M. L. Gentile):

however, that the *Codex Pisanus* of the Digest was known by the end of the eleventh century and that in the early decades of the twelfth century, there arose at Bologna a group of students of the Law who, by the technique they employed and the point of view they adopted, gave new life to the study of Law and made it, for the first time in the Middle Ages, a scientific pursuit. These men are known as the Glossators and the first of them is Irnerius.[3] 'Guarnerius, or as he was called later on, Irnerius, was undoubtedly the man who, at the dawn of the twelfth century founded the school of Bologna, the *alma mater* of legal science in the modern acceptation of the term.'[4] There are differences of opinion as to the details of his work, but the consensus is that he was truly the *lucerna iuris* of his times. The work of Irnerius and his followers was a new departure in legal studies since he applied himself to a close, critical and textual study of the sources of the law, and he began the systematic study of the whole *corpus iuris civilis* as the regular curriculum or the ordinary legal education.[5]

Irnerius probably lived between 1055 and 1130.[6] The variant spellings of his name attest the shadowy character of our knowledge of the man.[7] Most of his works are still in manuscript, but a beginning has been made in untangling the knotty problems of attribution that have long been discussed by legal

---

Maragone lived between 1110 and 1188 and was a prominent figure in the political life of Pisa, cf. A. Schaube, 'Bernardo Maragone doch der Verfasser der Annales Pisani,' *Neues Archiv der Gesellschaft für ältere deutsche Geschichtskunde* 10 (1885) 141–161. H. Kantorowicz, 'Ueber die Entstehung der Digestenvulgata,' *Zeitschrift der Savigny-Stiftung für Rechtsgeschichte, Rom. Abt.* [hereafter cited as ZRGRom.] 30 (1909) 203: 'Die Erzählung, dass die Hs. in Amalfi gelegen habe, dann 1135 (oder 1137) von den Pisanern erbeutet . . . ist Legende.'

[3] The testimony of Odofredus as to Irnerius having been a teacher of the *artes liberales* before he turned to the study of the law is accepted by Savigny IV, 10–11 and III, 427. Odofredus said: 'Dominus Yr. (Irnerius) qui fuit apud nos lucerna iuris i.e. primus qui docuit in civitate ista. Nam primo coepit studium esse in civitate ista in artibus . . . Sed dominus Yr. dum doceret in artibus in civitate ista . . . coepit per se studere in libris nostris, et studendo coepit docere in legibus et ipse fuit maximi nominis et fuit primus illuminator scientiae nostrae et quia primus fuit qui fecit glosas in libris nostris, vocamus eum lucernam iuris' (*In Dig. vetus*, L. 6 *de iust. et iure*). Cf. Savigny IV, 11, testimony of *Chronicon Urspergense* as to the influence of the Countess Matilda on the direction of Irnerius' studies. This background of Irnerius in the *artes* is a pregnant source for our interest in the origin of the *accessus* technique among the jurists. Fitting made a great deal of the study of law in the rhetorical schools of the Middle Ages, particularly the *genus iudiciale*; cf. H. Fitting, *Die Anfänge der Rechtsschule zu Bologna* (Berlin 1888) 92; cf. however the serious restrictions to this view in H. Kantorowicz, 'A Medieval Grammarian on the Sources of the Law,' *Revue d'histoire du droit (Tijdschrift voor Rechtsgeschiedenis)* 15 (1937) 37–39 and ZRGRom. 33 (1912) 417, 436.

[4] H. Kantorowicz, *Studies in the Glossators of the Roman Law* (Cambridge 1938) 33. (Hereafter cited as: Kantorowicz, *Glossators*.)

[5] H. Rashdall, *The Universities of Europe in the Middle Ages* (New edition, F. M. Powicke–A. B. Emden, Oxford 1936) I, 121 and Kantorowicz, ZRGRom. 31 (1910) 50.

[6] Kantorowicz, *Glossators* 33 and ZRGRom. 31, 14.

[7] Thus: Warnerius, Wernerius, Guarnerius, Gernerius, Irnerius, Hirnerius, Yrnerius. Cf. Savigny IV, 15.

scholars.[8] Irnerius and his pupils wrote *glossae*, a method of interlinear and marginal comments on specific words and points of the law. The method was not new as it had been used in the study of Lombard and Roman law in earlier centuries, as well as in grammatical commentaries.[9] The new feature of the Bolognese school was the consistent application of the glossatorial method to the law books of Justinian, and the widening of its scope so as to serve as an instrument of dialectical reasoning and systematic presentation. Especially the latter type of glosses gradually grew into independent treatises on a section or on a whole book of the law, and the result was known as a *summa*.[10] Rogerius, one of the pupils of Irnerius, appears to have been the first of the glossators to compose a formal *summa*,[11] but we possess some introductions which later were prefixed to *summae*, from the period that preceded Rogerius. One such *exordium*, if not by Irnerius himself, at least merits the designation *secundum Irnerium*.[12] This *exordium* contains a *materia Codicis* which is a form of the *accessus* that we have already seen used by the grammarians. It is clear that it is the same thing as the *accessus ad auctores*, with some adaptations to the needs of the glossators. This technique is to be found in the works of all of the twelfth-century glossators. The question of the *exordia* to the legal *summae* has lately been studied with remarkable perspicacity by Kantorowicz in the work which proved to be his last and what follows will, in large measure, be based on his statements and suggestions.[13] It will be helpful here to have before us an example of a legal *accessus* as a basis for comparison as to structure and for some idea of the value of this technique in the studies of the glossators of Roman law.

Idem Bulgarus super codice. Nota nominis excellentiam.
Quae sit *materia* Justiniani in opere hoc, videndum est; ad quod scire oportet quod Justinianus communem habet materiam cum aliis principibus, habet etiam propriam et

---

[8] Kantorowicz, *Glossators* is an edition of Brit. Mus. *Royal* MS 11. B. XIV which contains forty-one pieces of legal writings of the twelfth century by Irnerius and his followers, accompanied by a commentary on the glossators that is always illuminating and frequently brilliant. For an extensive review of this work see S. Kuttner, 'Zur neuesten Glossatorenforschung,' *Studia et Documenta Historiae et Iuris* 6 (Romae 1940) 275–319.

[9] Savigny III, 561–4 and C. Thurot, 'Doctrines grammaticales' (*supra*, p. 11 n. 22) 103, note 1.

[10] S. Kuttner, *Repertorium der Kanonistik (1140–1234): Prodromus corporis glossarum* (Città del Vaticano 1937) 123–4 and E. M. Meijers, 'Sommes, Lectures et Commentaires,' *Atti del Congresso Internazionale di Diritto Romano* I (Bologna/Roma 1934) 433.

[11] Odofredus *in Dig. vetus*, L. 1. *de transact.* 'Dominus Rogerius . . . contra dixit . . . in summa sua quam fecit super codice et fuit prima summa quae umquam fuerit facta . . .' quoted by Savigny IV, 214 a; and Kantorowicz, *Glossators* 149–180. This work now known as the *Summa Trecensis* was edited by Fitting (*Summa Codicis des Irnerius*, 1894) and attributed to Irnerius. Kantorowicz proves that Rogerius was the author, while Meijers, *Tijdschr. voor Rechtsgesch.* 17 (1939/40) 119–21 assigns the *Summa* to the School of Martinus.

[12] Kantorowicz, *Glossators* 46–48; 233–239. It is inscribed 'Super eodem Garnerius' in the London MS.

[13] *Op. cit.* 37–67.

singularem. Intentionem similiter communem et propriam. Sic etiam de utilitate dicendum est. [*Divisio sequentium*]

Communis materia omnium principum est equitas inconstituta; ius approbatum; vel illud quod pro lege et iure servatur, i.e. legitime voluntates contrahentium et ultimae voluntates deficientium.

Intendunt super equitate rudi eam eruere, erutam erigere, erectam subditis conservandum iniungere. Super iure iam fixo sic intendunt: quandoque rescribendo quandoque promulgando. Super.eo quod pro lege et iure servatur: quandoque ampliando ut in senatus consulto Macedoniano quo prohibitum est mutuam pecuniam dari filio familias, set et principes voluerunt idem esse in nepote. Coartant: cum filio familias alibi degenti causa studiorum mutuam pecuniam dari concedunt. Interpretantur: quandoque institutionem esse, ubi non fuit institutio, ut de illo, qui instituit ut filium, qui non erat filius; similiter interpretantur conditionem extitisse, que non extitit, ut 'si nuberit filio Anthylii'; quandoque non extitisse cum extitit, ut de illo qui hereditatem restituere iussus, si sine testamento decederet, relictis liberis non restituit. Hec omnia faciunt ad iustitiam respicientes, nunc primam, nunc secundam, nunc ad tertiam et quartam, quandoque ad questionem iuris sive nominis sive factisese referentes. Prima est, que, ex quo homines fuerunt, iussa est iustitia, ut Dominum colere, parentes revereri; secunda, que per se considerata iniustitia videtur, ad aliud relata apparet esse iustitia; tertia de litibus decidendis et causis terminandis; quarta de legibus condendis. De questione iuris, nominis et facti manifesta sunt exempla.

Ad hunc *finem* omnes spectant: errantes docere, rebelles eohibere, omnes bonos efficere tum metu penarum tum exhortatione premiorum.

Singularis et propria Justiniani *materia* sunt ipse principales constitutiones in tribus codicibus inconvenienter posite.

Intendit eas per diversa volumina dispersas quam plurima similitudine nec non diversitate vacillantes in unum codicem suo felici nomine decorandum reducere et omni vitio purgare.

Utilitas est, ut illa multitudinis confusione relicta ex uno solummodo codice Justiniani sc. constitutiones imperiales ad lites decidendas et causas terminandas facilius et commodius petantur.

Ethices est.

Set antequam ad eas tractandas veniat, premittuntur tres constitutiones, que etiam vicem proemiorum retinent.[14]

This *materia Codicis*, as these introductions were called by the legists, is by Bulgarus, one of the 'Four Doctors'. The other three are Martinus, Jacobus and Hugo. These men were prominent in the school at Bologna and in the affairs of the time, about the middle of the twelfth century, and it is very probable that they were the actual pupils of the master, Irnerius.[15] Bulgarus was the most famous of the four and he was born some time before 1100, his writings were composed between 1115 and 1165 and he is said to have died in 1166. His eloquence won for him the title of *os aureum*, the Chrysostom of the Jurists.[16] After these, there appear the names of Joannes Bassianus and Rogerius, the former a pupil of Bulgarus, and Rogerius, a pupil of Martinus. Joannes in turn taught the famous Azo, who attained an extraordinary renown for his glossatorial work. There was a proverb: 'Chi non ha Azzo, non vada a palazzo'

[14] *Op. cit.* 233–239.

[15] Savigny IV, 70, citing Radevicus, *De gestis Friderici* I, 2, 5 as follows: 'Habensque quatuor iudices, videlicet Bulgarum, Martinum, Jacobum, Hugonem, viros disertos, religiosos et in Lege doctissimos, Legumque in civitate Bononiensi Doctores et multorum auditorum praeceptores.' Cf. Kantorowicz, *Glossators* 68–69.

[16] Savigny IV, 82 and Kantorowicz, *Glossators* 68–70.

(He who does not know Azo, does not go to the Court).[17]   Accursius comes last in this list and his work came to be known as the *Glossa ordinaria*, in that his work was the common source for knowledge of the teaching of all of the Glossators.   Accursius died in 1263 and with him the school of the Glossators comes to an end.[18]

The *materia* given above is considered by Kantorowicz as the authentic work of Bulgarus, although it does not seem to have been the actual introduction to a *summa Codicis*, since there is no evidence that Bulgarus composed such a work. Hence it was probably written as a gloss on the opening words of the *Codex*.[19] The first *Summa Codicis* is that known as *Summa Trecensis*, which was written by Rogerius as a first draught about 1150.   Another is the work called by Kantorowicz *Summa Londiniensis*.[20]   Rogerius wrote another *Summa* about 1160, an elaboration of the *Summa Trecensis* of a decade earlier.[21]   There is a *Summa* by Placentinus written in 1175[22] and one by Joannes Bassianus about 1180.[23] The *Summa* of Azo was composed between 1208 and 1210.[24]   Each one of these in chronological order made use of the *summa* which preceded him in organizing his *materia codicis*, and the specimen we have given from Bulgarus is a representative example of the calibre of this introductory technique among the students of Roman Law.   The *materia secundum Irnerium* as discovered and edited by Kantorowicz was in a rather disordered state and he rearranged it, placing the items of the *materia* in a structure similar to that found in the *materia* of Bulgarus.[25]   His final opinion seems to be that the work is a redaction by some pupil of Irnerius, taken down from the lecture notes of the master.[26]   The growth of the technique of the *materia* in the hands of successive practitioners among the jurists is particularly striking under the heading of *intentio communis*.   First of all, it should be noted that this distinction of *materia*, *intentio* and *utilitas* into *communis* and *propria* (or *singularis* or *specialis*)[27] is a personal adaptation of the jurists, as it is not found in grammatical *accessus*.   In discussing the general purpose of all legislators, many were the suggestive ideas that arose which had a strong influence on the development of legal thinking in the twelfth century.   Of *intentio communis*, Kantorowicz says:

'This paragraph . . . which in Irnerius' *materia* had been quite short, occupies exactly one half of the whole *materia* in Bulgarus, three quarters in Rogerius and Placentinus, and two thirds in Joannes (Bassianus) and Azo.'[28]

---

[17] CMH V, 737.

[18] Kantorowicz, *Note* in: Beryl Smalley, *The Study of the Bible in the Middle Ages* (Oxford 1941) 36–38.

[19] Kantorowicz, *Glossators* 41–46.

[20] Brit. Mus. *Royal* MS 15. B. IV; cf. Kantorowicz, *op. cit.* 43, 6a.

[21] *Supra*, p. 16 n. 11 and Kantorowicz, *op. cit.* 125–133; text: Savigny, IV 524.

[22] G. Pescatore, *Miscellen, Beiträge zur mittelalterlichen Rechtsgeschichte*, Heft 2 (Berlin 1889); cf. Savigny IV, 543.

[23] Kantorowicz, *op. cit.* 44.

[24] *Ibid.* 44; Savigny V, 1–44; *Azonis Summa Aurea* (Lyon 1557).

[25] Kantorowicz, *op. cit.* 59–65.

[26] *Ibid.* 47; Kuttner, *Glossatorenforschung* 281.

[27] See the text of Bulgarus, *supra*, pp. 16–17.

[28] Kantorowicz. *op. cit.* 44–46.

On this topic, the lengthy analysis of Kantorowicz is most illuminating, showing as it does the results of further researches by later glossators into the text of the law, from which they drew more examples to illustrate the end and object of their science. The growing assurance with which they treat of this matter is a sign of the maturity and seriousness of their study of the law. It should also be mentioned that there is evidence of mere copying under some headings, where we find the exact phrasing of an earlier work repeated in that of a pupil.

The importance of this technique used in the introductions to the legal writings of the glossators was very great and on this matter we may be pardoned a rather long quotation from Kantorowicz:

> The various aspects which form their system afforded so many *loci* for the evolution of those sides of the science of law which the glossators in their mainly theoretical and dogmatic attitude, were inclined to neglect. The *materia* (in the narrower sense of subject-matter) suggested ideas on the basic divisions of the law and on the theory of the sources, particularly the problem of law and equity. The *modus tractandi*, generally combined with the *intentio* was considered the proper place for the discussion of the rules of interpretation and other questions of method. *Utilitas* (or *finis*) led to speculations on the purpose and function of law in general. The *pars philosophiae* was automatically classified as *ethica* but even this superficial treatment had the advantage of reminding the budding medieval lawyer that the civil law was more than a jungle of technicalities. Finally the *causa operis* (also treated under the heading *auctor, origo, occasio* and combined with *nomen*), tempted the glossators to make some elementary historical investigations. Thus the *materiae* represent the modest but venerable *incunabula* of General Jurisprudence. [29]

Kantorowicz compiled a chart of the use of the various items of this technique to be found in eight medieval writings: those of Irnerius, Bulgarus, *Summa Trecensis*, *Summa Londiniensis*, Rogerius, Placentinus, Joannes Bassianus and Azo. The seven items used in the *materia* are: *Divisio totius materiae, Nomen operis, Divisio sequentium, Materia–Intentio–Utilitas communis, Materia–Intentio–Utilitas specialis, Pars philosophiae* and *Continuatio*. In the eight works mentioned above, *Divisio totius materiae* is found only in Placentinus and *Pars philosophiae* is lacking in *Summa Londiniensis* and Rogerius.[30]

In his analysis of the origin of this technique of *materia*, Kantorowicz shows himself very well informed on the extent of the practice in medieval literature. He is aware of the existence of the *accessus* among the grammarians and he suspects its further extension. He stresses particularly the fact that the juristic *materiae* differed from the grammatical *accessus* in that the former are often preceded by some remarks of the commentator on his own personal work, the history of law, a protestation of humility etc., before going on to treat of the work at hand. Kantorowicz also shows that the technical term for the practice among the jurists was *Materia*, while other writers used such terms as *Prologus, Principium, Accessus, Praefatio, Praeludium, Prooemium, Introitus, Exordium*

---

[29] *Ibid.* 37–38. In the anonymous 'Juris peritie operam dare volentibus' (edited by Fitting, *Juristische Schriften des früheren Mittelalters* [Halle 1876] 145) an alternative is offered to the *pars philosophiae*, '. . . in hoc quod tractat de interpretatione verborum supponitur loice' (*sic*).

[30] *Ibid.* 51.

and *Preparatoria*.[31]   He gives no exact references for these names and it may be doubted whether all of them are the titles of precisely the type of introduction we are studying.   He suggests that the choice of *Materia* by the jurists was a *denominatio a potiori*.   'Of all the points mentioned above in the *accessus institutionum* the most important for the reader was obviously the subject-matter, the *materia*.'[32]   This seems to be rather an infelicitous choice of proof since the writing in question is called an *accessus* and not a *materia*, and further, the bulk of that introduction is concerned with the *intentio* and not with the *materia*. It would be of more pertinence here, to take cognizance of the predominant interest of the writer of the piece, and not of that of the reader.   A point which may possibly be suggestive is the fact that the word *accessus* appears to have had a technical meaning in law in several different contexts and this might have deterred the jurists from using it here.[33]   Struck by the consistent use of the *materia* among the glossators, Kantorowicz says: 'Such a uniformity presupposes a legally binding rule or an authoritative example or a constant tradition (not necessarily juristic) handed down from antiquity.   In the case of the legistic *exordia* all three were given.'[34]   He then cites from Gaius and from the Code itself which opens with the words: 'Juri operam daturus prius nosse oportet, unde nomen iuris descendat.'   Thirdly he cites a gloss of Martinus on the Institutes beginning: 'Morem recte scribentium servans Justinianus prologum premittit in quo lectores attentos, dociles et benevolos reddit.'   Several of the glossators refer to the fact that they are following in this last item 'morem aliorum auctorum' and Kantorowicz mentions this precept of the rhetoricians as to an *exordium* of a speech, citing Martianus Capella, Cassiodorus, Isidore and Boethius.[35]

At this point it must be said that an attempt to trace the origin of this type of conventionalized introduction by citing the precept of all of the ancient rhetoricians on the *exordium* is very probably fallacious—because the need for *lectores attenti*, *dociles*, and *benevoli* suggests a reason why a writer might feel the need of opening his work with some kind of an *exordium*, but not precisely with the kind of prologue that is in question here.   Further, Kantorowicz is perhaps over-simplifying the matter when he says: 'Boethius rests, of course, on Aristotle, especially on his theory of the four causes or principles (αἰτίαι, ἀρχαί), the *causa efficiens materialis formalis* and *finalis*, as the schoolmen said.'[36]   There does not seem to be any *direct* evidence of a connection between Aristotle and the *materia-accessus* technique; any reasonable man would want to know about a particular work just about the same things that Aristotle, in his Metaphysics, found adequate as an explanation of reality.   As a matter of fact, the school-

---

[31] *Ibid.* 38.

[32] *Ibid.* 39; the *Accessus Institutionum* opens: 'Sicut et in aliis libris ita in libris legum quedam requiruntur: materia, modus tractandi, intentio, utilitas, cui parti philosophiae supponatur, causa operis.'

[33] *Encycl. Brit.* I (11th ed.) 113.

[34] Kantorowicz, *op. cit.* 39–40.

[35] *Ibid.* 40.

[36] *Ibid.* 41.

men of the thirteenth century did reduce the *accessus* to the four causes, but that is no proof that originally the technique came from the four causes.

Kantorowicz devotes a separate discussion to the question of the *materiae Institutionum* since he finds that the literature on this matter has not been sufficiently explored as yet to warrant a chart of the use of the *materiae* as he had been able to do for the *materiae Codicis*.[37] However, in spite of the varying forms in which the *exordia* to the Institutes appear, the conclusion is warranted that the *materia* prefixed to that book is substantially the same as that used in the former case.   It will suffice for our purposes here to underline the fact that this type of introduction was to be found in this section also of the studies of the twelfth-century jurists, and apparently in the work of all of the glossators.

Before the recent book of Kantorowicz the only extended study of the juristic *materiae* was that made by Hermann Fitting,[38] whose concern was mainly with the *materiae Institutionum* and specifically with those to be found in a Prague Fragment which he edited.   Fitting's ideas have long been well known in juristic circles, particularly his persuasion that the school of Bologna was by no means a new development in the study of Roman Law in the Middle Ages, but that Bologna was merely the heir of a long period of intensive juristic studies which he, at times, would seem to trace in an uninterrupted line back to the times of Justinian.[39]   Consequently, Fitting tried to prove that the *materiae* of his Prague Fragment were to be dated many centuries before the opening of the school at Bologna and one of his most important proofs of that was the fact that the technique of the *materia* was to be found in his MS and also in the works of Boethius in the sixth century, and in the Greek predecessors of Boethius.

---

[37] *Ibid.* 50–58.

[38] *Juristische Schriften* (*supra*, p. 19 n. 29). *Cod. Prag. Metr.* J. LXXIV. On the contents of this MS cf. Kantorowicz, *op. cit.* 52–53.

[39] Fitting, *Die Anfänge* (*supra*, p. 15 n. 3) *passim*, and *Juristische Schriften* 88–107; the latter work was reviewed by Bruns, ZRGRom. 13 (1878) 105–120 who said: 'Ich glaube, dass hier Fitting seine alten Lieblinge wieder etwas überschätzt, wenn er eine vollständige Continuität zwischen ihnen und den Glossatoren annimmt und gerade daraus das Räthsel der plötzlichen Grösse der Glossatorenwissenschaft erklären will.' In the same volume (196–204), Mommsen discussed the textual portion of Fitting's exposition and 'disposed of it, once for all.' Fitting published a rejoinder to the two foregoing in the same volume, 'Ein Wort der Vertheidigung' (285–310) in which he reiterated his textual and historical arguments in support of his favorite view, mentioning traces of juristic studies, back to St. Gregory the Great. Later, Max Conrat (Cohn), *Geschichte und Quellen und Literatur des römischen Rechts im früheren Mittelalter* (Leipzig 1891) 155–156 showed the Prague Fragment to be a work of the twelfth century. Kantorowicz, *Glossators*, thus sums up: 'His arguments were in part textual, in part historical. The introductions, he declared, had used a text of the Digest which is independent of the Pisan (afterwards Florentine), and therefore of the school of Bologna; they follow the rules set up by the ancient rhetors and therefore must have been written in their epoch or connected with them by an unbroken juristic tradition. The textual part of the arguments was instantly disposed of, once for all, by Mommsen. The historical argument is like gazing reverently at the Doric columns of the *Brandenburger Tor* and then concluding that it must have been built in the times of Solon or that the Doric style had always been cultivated on the banks of the Spree.' Cf. also Kuttner, *Glossatorenforschung* 282 and note 12.

His mistake lay in jumping to the conclusion that because it was to be found in
Boethius, his MS must have been written in the time of Boethius, when in fact,
all that could be proven was that the *terminus post quem* for the jurists was the
death of Boethius.   Thus he states his point:

Nun war es schon bei den griechischen Commentatoren des Aristoteles eine feststehende
Forderung, dass jedes Werk philosophischen Inhaltes (und dazu werden . . . die juristischen
Werke gerechnet) mit der Definition und ihrer Erläuterung und mit der Erörterung einer
gewissen Anzahl bestimmter Fragen nach Zweck, Nützlichkeit, Echtheit, Grund der
Ueberschrift u. dgl. beginnen müsse.   Durch den Einfluss dieser Schule und namentlich des
besonders von Boetius so hoch geschätzten Porphyrius wurde die gleiche Regel auch nach
dem Abendlande verpflanzt und gerade im sechsten Jahrhundert allgemein befolgt.[40]

He then cites the opening section of Boethius' dialogue *In Porphyrii Isagogen*:

Sex omnino . . . magistri in omni expositione praelibant.   Praedocent enim quae sit cu-
iuscumque operis intentio, quod apud illos σκοπός vocatur; secundum, quae utilitas, quod a
Graecis χρήσιμον appellatur; tertium qui ordo, quod τάξιν vocant; quartum, si eius cuius
esse opus dicitur, germanus propriusque liber est, quod γνήσιον interpretari solent; quintum,
quae sit eius operis inscriptio, quod ἐπιγραφήν Graeci nominant.   In hoc etiam quod intentionem cuiusque libri insollerter interpretarentur, de inscriptione quoque operis apud
quosdam minus callentes haesitatum est.   Sextum est id dicere, ad quam partem philosophiae cuiuscunque libri ducatur intentio, quod Graeca oratione dicitur εἰς ποῖον μέρος
φιλοσοφίας ἀνάγεται.   Haec ergo omnia in quolibet philosophiae libro quaeri convenit
atque expediri.[41]

As another link in his chain of reasoning, Fitting quoted the *Liber Papiensis*,
a work of the eleventh century which has a form of the *materia*, albeit a defec-
tive one, in that the only points treated are: *Intentio, utilitas* and *ad quam
partem philosophiae supponatur*.[42]   This piece is found at the head of a collection of Lombard Capitularies.   Fitting then moved on to the certain works of
twelfth-century glossators and felt sure that he had established the continuity
of law studies all through the Middle Ages.   However little he proved with
regard to the Prague Fragment —and the writings were later seen to be works
of the twelfth century —he did a distinct service to those who are interested
in the career of the *accessus*, in pointing to its ancient origin.

b) *Canon Law*

Paralleling, though somewhat behind the study of Roman Law at Bologna
in the twelfth century, we find Canon Law coming to the stature of an exact
science in the person of Gratian, whose *Concordia discordantium canonum* was
written there between 1139 and 1142.[43]   Up to the time of Gratian the materials

[40] *Juristische Schriften* 95.

[41] Boethii *In Isagogen Porphyrii Commenta, editionis primae* I, 1 (ed. S. Brandt, CSEL
48, Vindobonae 1906); Fitting 96.

[42] *Liber Legis Langobardorum Papiensis dictus*, MGH SS IV, 290 (ed. A. Boretius, 1875);
Fitting 99.

[43] J. F. von Schulte, *Die Geschichte der Quellen und Literatur des Canonischen Rechts
von Gratian bis auf die Gegenwart* (Stuttgart, I 1875; II 1877) I, 46–75; J. de Ghellinck,
S.J., *Le Mouvement théologique du XIIᵉ siècle* (Paris 1914) 277–346; S. Kuttner, 'The Father
of the Science of Canon Law,' *Jurist*, 1 (1941) 1–19.

of Canon Law were to be found with difficulty in the many voluminous collections made at different times and places with different principles of selection and arrangement, but never before had an attempt been made at a comprehensive compilation of all this vast material. The work of Gratian, however, was not merely that of compilation, but, as he indicated in the title he gave to the book, it was an attempt to bring order and system to what must have been a bewildering confusion and a mass of contradictions. The *Concordia* is a milestone in the intellectual growing-up of the Middle Ages. He divided his work into three parts; each of these is made up of minor units in which Gratian introduces canonical problems, presents the canons which seem to answer the given problem in one way or another, and solves in dialectical fashion the apparently contradictory evidence he had adduced. Marked simply with a paragraph sign, these observations, objections and solutions came to be known as the *Dicta Gratiani*.[44]

Proximity to the school of Roman Law at Bologna inevitably caused the canonists to be influenced by the civilians and it would seem that some of the men who have come down to us as pupils of Gratian had also studied under some of the Four Doctors.[45] Hence it is not surprising that we find the technique of the *materia* among the canonists. For fifty years after the publication of Gratian's work, which came to be known as the *Decreta*, there was an industrious group of *Magistri Decretorum* who, first in numerous glosses on the *Decreta*, then in *Summae*, systematic text-books or detailed commentaries, furthered and explained the work of Gratian. These men worked between the forties and the eighties of the twelfth century and after the last of them, Huguccio, about 1190, the intense activity in interpreting the *Decreta* came to a standstill.[46] It is with this group of Decretists that we will be concerned in our study of the use of the *materia* by the canonists; a few examples will be given

[44] *Decretum Magistri Gratiani*, ed. A. Friedberg (Leipzig 1879); *Prolegomena* on the sources used by Gratian, xix–lxxv. As to the formal division of the work, the distribution of part ii into thirty-six *Causae*, with a number of *quaestiones* each, is original, but the formal division of parts i and iii, and of *Causa* 33, *quaestio* 3, into *distinctiones* is not. Cf. F. Gillmann, *Archiv für katholisches Kirchenrecht* 112 (1932) 504 ff.

[45] E.g., Stephen of Tournai: cf. J. Warichez, *Etienne de Tournai et son temps* (Tournai/Paris 1936) 19.

[46] S. Kuttner, 'Bernardus Compostellanus Antiquus, A Study in the Glossators of the Canon Law,' *Traditio*, 1 (1943) 279–285. 'For the moment, apparently not much was left to be said about Gratian's work in the way of commenting and glossing. No other Summa appeared in Bologna and the only writings published on Gratian during the nineties . . . were . . . intended for other purposes than that of adding to the exegetic discussion . . . The slackening of the decretist production was due to a fundamental innovation in the study of canon law. Hitherto, the new decretals of the recent popes . . . had been used occasionally as *extravagantes* (i.e. *decretales extra decreta vagantes*) by the Bolognese school . . . But now for the first time a collection of decretals was formally made the subject of lecturing, apart from the *Decreta*: the *Breviarium extravagantium* by Bernard Balbi of Pavia, composed between 1188 and 1192, and which was later called the *Compilatio prima*. . . . It established the pattern for all other decretal collections and decretalist science to come. For Bologna then, the prevailing interest in the interpretation of the new decretals . . . explains, in our opinion, the stagnation of decretist production after the time of Huguccio.'

among the later decretalists merely to show that the practice continued and, very probably, is to be found in the later commentators on Canon Law.

The first of the pupils of Gratian is Paucapalea (1140–1148)[47] and he is followed by Rolandus Bandinelli, the future Pope Alexander III,[48] who wrote *Stroma ex decretorum corpore carptum*, sometime before 1148, and is also known as a theologian. The third is Rufinus,[49] later Bishop of Assisi; his *Summa Decretorum* was written in the late fifties (1157–1159) of the twelfth century. From France Stephen of Tournai[50] came to Bologna to study law under Bulgarus and Gratian. He returned to his native Orléans, became abbot of St. Geneviève in Paris and in 1192, Bishop of Tournai. A theologian as well as a jurist he often cites Peter Lombard and his three predecessors from Bologna. There follows John of Faenza (Joannes Faventinus)[51] who enjoyed a very widespread influence, judging from the MSS of his *Summa* which he wrote after 1171. Sicardus of Cremona[52] was an Italian who studied law at Bologna, later went to Mainz for a few years, and became Bishop of his native city in 1185. His *Summa* is dated 1179–1181. The last and the greatest of the *Magistri Decretorum* is Huguccio[53] who wrote a *Summa* around 1188, which unfortunately is still in MSS and hence unavailable as evidence in the matter of the *materia*. However, in any enumeration of the canonical glossators he cannot be omitted. Of the French school of Decretists, we will include in our chart of *materiae* the anonymous *Summa Parisiensis* (about 1170).[54]

With Bernard Balbi of Pavia begins the new era in canonical study, the age of the Decretalists, represented in our chart by his *Summa titulorum decre-*

[47] Schulte, *Quellen (supra,* p. 22 n. 43) I, 109; Kuttner, *Repertorium* 125–6; 12; see also *Traditio* 1, 280 note 9. Text: Schulte, *Die Summa des Paucapalea* (Giessen 1890).

[48] Schulte, *Quellen,* I, 114–118; Kuttner, *Repertorium* 127–129; 56; 12; Text: F. Thaner, *Summa Magistri Rolandi* (Innsbruck 1874) and A. M. Gietl, *Die Šentenzen Rolands* (Freiburg im Breisgau 1891).

[49] Schulte, *Quellen* I, 121–130 (incorrect); Kuttner, *Repertorium* 131–132; 12; *Traditio* 1, 280 note 10. Text: H. Singer, *Summa decretorum des Magister Rufinus* (Paderborn 1902, with an important introduction).

[50] Schulte, *Quellen* I, 133–136; Kuttner, *Repertorium,* 133–136; 12; *Traditio* 1, 282 note 20. Text: Schulte, *Die Summa des Stephanus Tornacensis über das Decretum Gratiani* (Giessen 1891), and text of the exordium: Schulte, *Quellen,* I, 251–255. There is a recent life by J. Warichez (*supra,* p. 23 n. 45).

[51] Schulte, *Quellen* I, 137–140; Kuttner, *Repertorium* 143–146; 145: 'Nicht als Autor im modernen Sinn, sondern als einflussreicher und wirksamer Vermittler der Lehren seiner Vorgänger ist Johannes also historisch zu würdigen.' Kuttner, *Traditio* 1, 281 note 11. Text, selections: Schulte, 'Die Glosse zum Dekret Gratians von ihren Anfängen bis auf die jüngsten Ausgaben,' *Denkschriften der kaiserlichen Akademie der Wissenschaften, Wien, Philosophisch-historische Classe* 21, 2 (1872) 40.

[52] Schulte, *Quellen* I, 143–145; Kuttner, *Repertorium* 150–153; portions of the text are to be found in Schulte, *Sitzungsberichte der kaiserlichen Akademie der Wissenschaften, Wien, Phil.-histor. Classe* 63 (1869) 337.—The *Summa* of Sicardus' somewhat older contemporary, Simon of Bisignano, dated 1177–1179 (Schulte I, 141–142; Kuttner, *Repertorium* 148f.; *Traditio* 1, 281 n. 12), is not available.

[53] M. Manitius, *Geschichte der lateinischen Literatur des Mittelalters* III, 191–193; Schulte, *Quellen* I, 156–170; Kuttner, *Repertorium* 155–160; *Traditio* 1, 283 notes 21 and 22.

[54] Schulte, *Sitzungsberichte Wien,* 64 (1870) 130; *Quellen* I, 224; Kuttner *Repertorium* 177. Text: *SBWien* 64, 119.

talium (ca. 1191–1198),[55] the *Summa Ambrosii*[56] and the *Summa Damasi* (both ca. 1210–1215).[57] The latter two *summae* are noteworthy in that they alone, of the *summae* here listed, include the *pars philosophiae* in their *materiae*. Apart from this detail there is a general uniformity in the handling of the schema by the canonists.

The differences between the canonists and the civilians flow from the nature of the work on which they were commenting. It will be apparent that the question of the authenticity of the work would be of no more pertinence here than with the civilians, since no one doubted that Justinian and Gratian were the *auctores* of the works attached to their names. The canonists, however, as a general rule were so completely theologically minded that they would not have included their work as a part of philosophy at all.[58] This becomes clear when we recall the close connection between the work of Gratian and that of Peter Lombard and the large theological section of the *Decreta*. Occasionally we find the refinement introduced by the civilians, of dividing the *materia*, *intentio* and *utilitas* into *communis* and *propria*. An example of such a distinction is to be found in Sicardus of Cremona who divides his *materia decretorum* in this fashion: '*Huius ergo canonici iuris* . . . materia, intentio, finis et iuris divisio . . . *Praeterea quae sit materia Gratiani*: intentio, causa intentionis, utilitas et distinctio libri.'[59] Rufinus, however, introduces a triple framework, giving three topics under *Jus*, two under *Canones* and five under *Gratianus*. A review of the adjoining chart will show that *materia*, *intentio* and *modus tractandi* are the normal elements to be found in the use of the *Materia* by the canonists. In most cases they apparently took the *utilitas* for granted and on this Rufinus says laconically: '*Quanta huius libri sit utilitas studiose et perseveranter legentibus apparebit.*'[60] Bernardus Papiensis was able to specify the good to be expected from its study: '*Utilitas patet quia per huius operis scientiam promtiores erimus ad consulendum, allegandum et diffiniendum.*'[61] And Ambrosius: '*Utilitas est, ut sciamus discernere inter equum et iniquum.*'[62] The *modus tractandi* is always the division of the text commented upon—threefold in the

----

[55] Schulte, *Quellen* I, 175–182; Kuttner, *Repertorium* 387–390; *Traditio* 1, 295; 299 n. 38. Text: *Bernardi Papiensis Faventini Episcopi Summa Decretalium* (ed. E. A. Laspeyres, Regensburg 1860).

[56] Kuttner, *Repertorium* 392–393, who quotes the opening lines of the *materia*: 'Formavit Deus hominem etc . . . Ex his igitur iam patet materia, liquet intentio, utilitas innotescit.' In *Glossatorenforschung* 281 note 10, he implies that the *Summa Ambrosii* also lists the item *cui parti philosophiae supponatur*. This unpublished passage reads in the MSS Venice, *Marc. lat.* IV. 25 and Fulda D. 10 (information supplied by Dr. Kuttner): 'Cum autem tres sint partes philosophie, sc. ethica, phisica et logica, . . . queritur cui parti philosophie subponatur. Et quidem ethice, quia tractat de moribus, sicut omnes libri alii iuris.'

[57] Kuttner, *Repertorium* 393–396; Schulte, 'Literaturgeschichte der Compilationes Antiquae,' *SBWien* 66 (1870) 139–140 gives the text. *Quellen* I, 194 n. 2.

[58] Kantorowicz, *Glossators* 37 note 4.

[59] Schulte, *SBWien* 63 (1869) 337.

[60] *Die Summa des Magister Rufinus* 5.

[61] *Bernardi Papiensis summa decretalium* (ed. Laspeyres) 2.

[62] MSS of Venice and Fulda (cf. note 56 *supra*). Ambrosius' source is here a gloss by Vincentius Hispanus (ed. Schulte, *SBWien* 66, 106f.).

case of Gratian's work, and fivefold in the collections of decretals since Bernardus Papiensis—with minor variations. The *intentio* is generally that implied in Gratian's title, to resolve the apparent contradictions between the different *decreta*, or, with the decretalists, to compile and arrange into proper *tituli* the decretals of the recent popes.[63] As to the subject matter the glossators all agree in saying that it is: *decreta* and *canones*,[64] or *decretales*.

CHART OF THE MATERIAE OF THE CANONISTS

[1] *Paucapalea* 1140–1148	[2] *Rolandus Band.* Ante 1148	[3] *Rufinus* 1157–1159

Materia
Intentio
 	
Modus tractandi
	Nomen
	Causa scribendi
	
	Quibus scripserit
	
	Materia
	
	Intentio
	
	Modus scribendi
		JURIS Intentio
		   qui potest. habet condendi
		     ius humanum et divinum
		   Utilitas
		CANONUM Intentio
		   Utilitas
		MAGISTRI GRATIANI Materia
		      Intentio
		      Modus tractandi
		      Utilitas
		      Titulus

[4] *Steph. Tornacens.* ca. 1165	[5] *Joan. Favent.* Post 1171	[6] *Summa Paris.* 1170	[7] *Sicardus* 1180

Materia
Intentio
Finis intentionis
Causa operis
Modus tractandi
Distinctio libri
	Intentio
	(Nomen)
	Materia
	(Divisio operis)
		Materia
		Intentio
			CANONICI IURIS Materia
			    Intentio
			    Finis
			    Divisio
			GRATIANI Materia
			    Intentio
			    Causa inten-
			      tionis
			    Utilitas
			    Distinctio libri

[8] *Bern. Papiensis* 1191–1198	[9] *Summa Ambrosii* 1210–1215	[10] *Summa Damasi* 1215
Nomen Materia Intentio Utilitas Ordo agendi	Intentio Materia Utilitas Pars philosophiae Modus agendi	Materia Intentio Utilitas Ordo agendi Pars philosophiae

[63] Damasus, *Summa*, gives a different *intentio*: '. . . ut metu poenarum in eis [sc. constitutionibus summorum pontificum] expressarum humana coerceatur audacia et iusti vivere possint in quiete' (Schulte, *SBWien* 66, 140).

[64] The consecrated phrase seems to have been 'Materia *sunt* canones . . .'; cf. F. Maassen, 'Ein Beitrag zur juristischen Literargeschichte des Mittelalters,' *SBWien* 24 (1857) 13 and Schulte, *Denkschriften* (*supra*, p. 24 n. 51) 7.

The most striking feature of the *materiae* of the canonists is that the *materia* is the concluding section of the *exordium*, which generally opens with a protestation of humility, stressing the inability of the writer to resolve all questions and to satisfy all classes of readers. Then follows a discussion of the origin of law, which is traced from the commandments given by God to Moses, the various enactments of the Old Testament, St. Paul, the councils of the Church, both general and provincial, which resulted in the collections of canons. The necessity of law is traced to human weakness and it is a sign of divine mercy that God has given us Law to guide us; all of which leads up to the fact, either, that Gratian in his work took all of this material as his *materia operis*,[65] or, that the new compilations after Gratian became necessary, 'quia non omnia poterant compaginari in corpore decretorum.'[66]

As an example of the method of treatment of a *materia decretorum* of the canonical Glossators we offer that of Stephen of Tournai which enjoyed a very widespread popularity in the Middle Ages.

Circa librum autem quem prae manibus habemus, haec attendenda sunt, scil. quae sit operis materia? quae ipsius intentio? quis finis intentionis? quae causa operis? quis modus tractandi? quae distinctio libri?

Compositorem huius operis recte dixerim Gratianum, non auctorem. Capitula namque a sanctis patribus edita in hoc volumine exposuit, i.e. ordinavit. Non eorum auctor vel conditor fuit, nisi forte quis eum auctorem ideo dicere velit, quoniam multa ex parte sua etiam distinguendo et exponendo sanctorum sententias in *paragraphis* suis ponit.

Huius *materia* sunt canones, decreta et decretales epistolae, quorum differentiam supra legisti. Auctoritates etiam sanctorum patrum, quae, quamvis potestatem condendi canones non habuerint, non minimum tamen locum in ecclesia habent.

Intentio eiusdem est, diversas diversorum patrum regulas, quae canones dicuntur, in unum colligere et contrarietates, quae in eis videntur occurrere, in concordiam revocare.

Finis, i.e. utilitas est, scire ecclesiastica negotia, de iure canonico tractare et tractata canonice definire.

Causa operis haec est: cum per ignorantiam ius divinum iam in desuetudinem devenerit et singulae ecclesiae consuetudinibus potius quam canonibus regerentur, periculosum id reputans Gratianus diversos codices conciliorum et patrum capitula continentes collegit, et, quae magis sibi necessaria causis decidendis videbantur, in hoc volumine comprehendit.

Modus tractandi hic est: primum ponit iuris distinctiones et differentias, deinde causam constitutionis legum et canonum, postea transit ad ordinem et numerum conciliorum, et quorum decreta quibus sint praeferenda. Postmodum ad dignitates et ordines ecclesiasticos accedit docens, quibus sint conferendae et qualiter in eis sit vivendum. De ordinibus etiam, quibus intervallis temporum sint largiendi, qualiter etiam lapsi reparentur. Tandem transit ad causas in quibus ostendit primo de accusationibus et testibus et ordine iudiciario, quis etiam modus in diversis ecclesiasticis negotiis sit habendus. Tandem ad coniugii causas veniens et ea sufficienter tractans in fine de ecclesiarum consecratione, de sacramento corporis et sanguinis domini, de baptismo et confirmatione supponit.

Distinguitur liber iste alias secundum diligentiam lectorum, alias secundum consuetudinem scriptorum. Lectores in tres partes distinguunt. Quod et Gratianus voluisse videtur. Prima pars usque ad causam symoniacorum extenditur, quam Gratianus per C et I distinctiones divisit. Secunda a prima causa usque ad tractatum de consecratione procedit, quae per XXXVI causas quaestionibus suis decisas distinguitur. Tertia a tractatu consecrationis usque ad finem, quam per V distinctiones secant. Harum primam ministeriis, secun-

---

[65] Cf. the *exordium* of Stephen of Tournai (ed. Schulte) 1.

[66] Cf. Ambrosius (Kuttner, *Repertorium* 393); Vincentius, *loc. cit.* (*supra*, p. 25 n. 62).

dam negotiis, tertiam ecclesiasticis deputat sacramentis. Scriptorum consuetudo librum
istum in quatuor partes distinguit, quarum unumquamque quartam appellant. Et primam
quidem a principio usque ad primam causam, quae est de symoniacis, secundam a prima
causa usque ad tertiam decimam quae sic incipit: 'Diocesani', tertiam usque ad XXVII,
quae est de matrimonio prima, quartam a XXVII usque ad finem libri ponunt.
    His praelibatis ad literam veniamus.[67]

From the general similarity of treatment of the *materia* technique by the
canonists and the civilians, it is possible that the former copied it from their
somewhat older contemporaries. However, there is one piece of evidence
which may point to a source of direct influence on the canonists. It is the
Epistola Burchardi episcopi Wormacensis written to Alpert, author of a work
De diversitate temporum, probably in 1022. Alpert had dedicated his work to
Burchard who was, from 1000 to 1025, when he died, Bishop of Worms.[68] An
extract from Burchard's letter follows:

In omni expositione auctorali et in quolibet libro, diversas sex causas quaeri convenit atque
expediri oportet, sicut in proemio editionis primae ysagogorum Porphyrii Severinus
[Boethius] prudentissimus doctor, Fabio exhortante, dicendo instituit: Primum inquit,
docent quae sit cuiusque operis intentio, secundo quae utilitas, tercio qui ordo, quarto si
eius cuius opus esse dicitur, germanus propriusque liber est; quinto quae sit eius inscriptio,
sextum est id dicere, ad quam partem philosophiae cuiuscunque libri ducatur intentio.[69]

Now Burchard had written his famous *Decretum*, which was one of the sources
used by Gratian, and it is certain that the glossators were familiar with that
work.[70] It is possible that they may also have known this letter, a slighter
work, to be sure, and one not directly connected with their studies, but, they
may have found it united to the more substantial work of Burchard. The
Decretum itself does not contain anything in the nature of an *exordium* or *materia*.[71] Burchard's acquaintance with the use of this introductory technique
as found in Boethius, however, may point to that sixth-century writer as one
of the sources by which the practice came into the schools of canon law.

[67] Schulte, *Quellen* I, 253–255.
[68] MGH SS IV, 701; A. Potthast, *Bibliotheca historica medii aevi*, I, 37; *Vita* by G. Waitz,
MGH *ibid.* 829–846.
[69] Cf. *supra*, p. 22 at n. 41. This letter is mentioned by Kantorowicz, *Glossators* 41.
[70] Schulte *Quellen* I, 44: 'Burchards Decretum: Dies ist die ausnahmlos allen Glossatoren des XII. Jahrhunderts bekannteste Sammlung, wie zahlreiche Citate in den Glossen
und Summen bekunden. Bei Rufin kommen sehr viele Citate aus ihm vor, einige bei
Stephanus, über 50 bei Simon de Bisiniano, viele bei Johannes Faventinus, mehrere bei
Sicardus, in der Summa Coloniensis, Parisiensis, über 50 in der Lipsiensis usw.' Cf. Conrat (*supra*, p. 21 n. 39) I, 261.
[71] Of the other sources of the *Decretum Gratiani* that were available none contains a
materia, cf. F. Maassen, 'Glossen des canonischen Rechts aus dem carolingischen Zeitalter,'
SBWien 84 (1877) 235–298; nor do we find anything pertinent in Ivo of Chartres, *Panormia*,
PL 161, 1042, or *Decretum, ibid.* 9; cf. J. R. Menu, *Recherches et nouvelle étude critique sur
les recueils de Droit Canon attribués à Yves de Chartres* (Paris 1880); P. Fournier, 'Les
collections canoniques attribuées à Yves de Chartres,' *Bibliothèque de l'Ecole des chartes*
57 and 58 (1896–97); Fournier–Le Bras, *Histoire des collections canoniques en occident* II
(Paris 1932) 55–114, 337; likewise Amalarius of Metz, *De officiis ecclesiasticis* (PL 105, 986),
Regula sanctimonialium (935), and *Regula canonicorum* (815).

III. THE PHILOSOPHERS

The quest of the fate of the *accessus* technique among the lawyers has led us to Boethius and especially to his *In Isagogen Porphyrii Commenta*. Equally, if not more, significant for our purpose is the fact that the source from which Boethius learned this technique, opens even more widely the horizons of the whole discussion. Well known is the ambition of Boethius of translating and harmonizing all of the writings of Plato and Aristotle, but this was rendered impossible by his early death, for treason, at the hands of Theoderic.[1] But, in the early years of the sixth century Boethius had apparently started on this gigantic project and his *In librum Aristotelis de interpretatione* is said to have been the first of his philosophical works. We know that he was working on the *In Categorias Aristotelis Commentarium* in 510 when burdened with the consular office, and he himself tells us that at that time, he had already written his commentary on the *Isagoge*.[2] Therefore, we may conclude that the work

---

[1] 'Ego omne Aristotelis opus quodcunque in manus venerit, in Romanum stilum vertens, eorum omnia commenta latina oratione perscribam, ut si quid ex logicae artis subtilitate, et ex moralis gravitate peritiae, et ex naturali acumine veritatis ab Aristotele conscriptum est, id omne ordinatum transferam, atque id quodam lumine commentationis illustrem, omnesque Platonis dialogos vertendo, vel etiam commentando, in latinam redigam formam. His peractis non equidem contempserim Aristotelis Platonisque sententiam in unam quodammodo revocare concordiam, et in his non ut plerique dissentire in omnibus, sed in plerisque quae sunt in philosophia maxime consentire demonstrem.' *In librum de interpretatione, secunda editio* II c. 3 (ed. C. Meiser [Leipzig 1877–80] II, 79–80).

On similar ambitions in the twelfth century, John of Salisbury remarked: 'Egerunt operosius Bernardus Carnotensis et auditores eius ut componerent inter Aristotelem et Platonem, sed eos tarde venisse arbitror et laborasse in vanum ut reconciliarent mortuos qui, quando in vita licuit, dissenserunt.' *Metalogicon* II, xvii (ed. C. C. J. Webb, Oxford 1929, p. 94). On Boethius see E. K. Rand, *The Founders of the Middle Ages* (Cambridge 1929) 156; H. Usener, *Anecdoton Holderi* (Bonn 1877); C. H. Coster, *The Iudicium Quinquevirale* (Cambridge, Med. Acad. Monographs X, 1935); William Bark, 'Boethius vs. Theoderic, Vindication and Apology,' *American Historical Review* 44 (1944) 410–426. On the popularity and influence of Boethius in the Middle Ages, see M. Grabmann, *Geschichte der scholastischen Methode* (Freiburg im Breisgau 1909) I, 148–177 and M. Baumgartner, *Die Philosophie des Alanus de Insulis* (Münster 1896) 12. Boethius was the principal source of knowledge of the logic of Aristotle up to the time of the reception of the complete *Organon* in the twelfth century.

[2] Boethius, *In Categorias Aristotelis* (PL 64, 201B): 'Etsi nos curae officii consularis impediunt quominus in his studiis omne otium plenamque operam consumimus, pertinere tamen videtur hoc ad aliquam rei publicae curam, elucubratae rei doctrina cives instruere.' And, the opening lines of the same commentary (159A): 'Expeditis his quae ad praedicamenta Aristotelis Porphyrii institutione digesta sunt, hos quoque commentarios....' Boethii *In Isagogen Porphyrii Commenta* (ed. S. Brandt, CSEL 48) xxvi–xxvii. A recent article by Lorenzo Minio-Paluello ('The genuine text of Boethius' translation of Aristotle's Categories,' *Medieval and Renaissance Studies* I, ii [London 1941–43] 151–177) denies the authenticity of the received text of Boethius' translation of the Categories of Aristotle. He believes that the translation accompanying the commentary of Boethius (PL 64, 159–294) is not that of Boethius, but a shorter version of some tenth-century translator who re-translated some passages from the Greek, and revised others because the text of Boethius was not complete originally, Boethius having omitted

from which we have cited his use of the *accessus* was written A.D. 508–509.[3]

This work survives in two editions, for the first of which Boethius used the translation made by Victorinus;[4] in the second edition, he re-translated from the Greek of Porphyry and expanded his commentary, with notable changes.[5] The introduction to the second edition is considerably curtailed. For, whereas in the first edition he enumerated six items, namely, *intentio, utilitas, ordo, an sit germanus eius cuius opus esse dicitur, inscriptio* and *ad quam partem philosophiae*, in the second he mentions only *intentio* and *utilitas*.[6] In his commentary on the Categories[7] of Aristotle he speaks of *intentio, utilitas, ordo*, and *pars philosophiae* and in his introduction to *De Interpretatione*[8] we find only *intentio* and *utilitas*. None of the other works of Boethius has this form of introduction.

When we seek, however, for the source used by Boethius in these commentaries from which he learned the use of the *accessus*—he does not use this term but calls the items he saw fit to discuss, *didascalica*—we are introduced to the voluminous works of the Alexandrian commentators on Aristotle, and in the case of that on the *Isagoge* of Porphyry, to the work of Ammonius, the son of Hermeias, Ἀμμωνίου Ἑρμείου ἐξήγησις τῶν πέντε φωνῶν.[9] Brandt, in his edition of

---

the parts not indispensable to his commentary; and also because scribes assumed that readers would have a continuous text at hand when reading the commentary and hence did not transcribe the *lemmata* in their entirety. The original text of Boethius, he believes, is to be found in MSS *Marcianus* Z. L. 497 and Paris B. N. *lat.* 2788, mainly because, in those places where the text of the commentary resumes the text of the *lemma*, the commentary agrees with these two MSS rather than with the received text. Hence he concludes that 'the version which up to now has been ascribed to Boethius partly belongs to the tenth century and therefore, there was a medieval translation of Aristotle into Latin at a much earlier date than is commonly supposed.' Cf. G. Théry, O.P., *Alexandre d'Aphrodise* (Bibliotèque Thomiste VII, Le Saulchoir 1926) 16.

[3] Boethius' works on the *quadrivium* (*Institutio arithmetica, Institutio musica, Ars geometrica*) seem to have been his earliest published works; cf. Brandt, CSEL 48, xxvii–xxix and *Excursus II*, lxxix–lxxxii; E. K. Rand, *Der dem Boethius zugeschriebene Traktat De fide catholica* (Jahrbücher für klassische Philologie, XXVI. Supplementbd. Leipzig 1901).

[4] CSEL 48, 4, 11–14: 'Rogo ut mihi explices id quod Victorinus orator sui temporis ferme doctissimus Porphyrii per Isagogen . . . dicitur transtulisse.' And, *ibid.* 347, 24–348, 1: 'Nos etiam, quoniam promissi operis portum tenemus atque huius libri seriem primo quidem ab rhetore Victorino, post vero a nobis Latina oratione conversam gemina expositione patefecimus. . . .'

[5] *Editio secunda* is one third longer; cf. Brandt, *op. cit.* xviii–xxvi.

[6] *Op. cit.* 143, 8–148, 12.

[7] PL 64, 159A–161C.

[8] *In lib. de interp.* (*supra*, p. 29 n. 1) I, 32; 34; II, 7, 13. On the importance of Boethius' work as a commentator, cf. Grabmann, *Geschichte* I, 159: 'Für uns handelt es sich hier nur, in ganz allgemeinen Umrissen die vorbildliche Bedeutung der Kommentare des Boethius zu Aristoteles und Porphyrius für die mittelalterliche Kommentierungsliteratur, speziell für die Aristotelesexegese, darzulegen. Im Einleitungskapitel zu seiner ersten Isagogeerklärung gibt Boethius im Anschlusse an griechischen Quellen die Richtpunkte an, die für die Erklärung einer philosophischen Schrift massgebend sind. Es sind . . . Gesichtspunkte, an der Hand welcher mittelalterliche Interpreten sich eine zu erläuternde Quellenschrift gründlich und nach allen Seiten besehen konnten.'

[9] Ammonius, *In Porphyrii Isagogen sive V voces* (ed. A. Busse, *Commentaria in Aristotelem Graeca* [*Academiae Litterarum Regiae Borussicae*] IV, iii, Berlin 1891). All citations

Boethius, has investigated the dependence of Boethius upon his Greek sources and he finds a manifold correspondence between the Greek and Latin works on the *Isagoge*. This is especially true, according to Brandt, of the *prooemia* to the two works and the conclusion is mandatory that Boethius' use of the *didascalica* is an adaptation of that of Ammonius.[10] The figure of Ammonius looms large in our knowledge of the later students of Aristotle and the list of his personal pupils and their students includes all the names of those who were interested in Aristotle in the fifth to the seventh centuries.[11] The versatile Ammonius seems to have lived around the end of the fifth century, and to have been famous as a Mathematician, Astronomer, Grammarian, Rhetorician and Philosopher.[12] The 'school' that he founded was diligent in its study of Aristotle and even the extant works are copious material for an estimate of their viewpoint and scholarship. Ammonius was apparently not a Christian, a fact that is of some significance, in view of the rather harsh views of Przychocki mentioned above.[13] Ammonius was a pupil of Proclus who died in 485 and so, on chronological grounds, it is possible that Boethius could have used his work.[14] On this point, however, Brandt finds no lack of certainty.

The first of the pupils of Ammonius was Simplicius whose *floruit* is placed around the year 500.[15] In his voluminous commentary on the Categories of

---

of these commentators will be referred to as: ALRB, volume and page, of each edition. Cf. the valuable note of Brandt in his edition of Boethius, *Excursus I*, lxxviii–ix, which first directed this writer to the sources of Boethius among the Alexandrian commentators.

[10] *Ibid.* xxii–xxvi. Cf. *Excursus A, infra*, pp. 38–40.

[11] PWK I, 1863 (Freudenthal): 'In der That war er ein kenntnisreicher, vielseitiger, und . . . auch ein besonnener und vorurteilsfreier Gelehrter, der zugleich als Mathematiker, Astronom, Grammatiker, Rhetor und Philosoph sich hervorthat. . . . Fest steht schon heute, dass auch jüngere Commentare zum Organon, wie die des Olympiodor, Johannes Philoponus, Elias, David, Nikephorus, Blemides, Leo Magentinus u. a. mittelbar oder unmittelbar auf Ammonius' Erklärungen zurückgehen.'

[12] Christ–Schmid–Stählin, *Geschichte der griechischen Literatur* II, 1066–7: 'Die erhaltenen Aristoteleskommentare des Ammonius verraten keine besondere geistige Selbständigkeit, aber vielseitige Gelehrsamkeit und verhältnismässig nüchternen Sinn, und für seine Lehrbegabung spricht die grosse Zahl seiner bedeutenden Schüler. Alle tüchtigeren Aristotelesexegeten des ausgehenden 5. Jhs. sind nämlich aus seiner Schule hervorgegangen; . . . auf Damaskios hat er weniger gewirkt, aber auf Simplicius, Asklepios v. Tralles, Olympiodorus den Jüngeren, Johannes Philoponus v. Kaiserea, ist seine Art übergegangen und auch die späteren stehen noch unter seinem Einfluss.' Cf. Busse, *op. cit.* xxxv; Zeller, *Die Philosophie der Griechen* (3. Aufl. Leipzig 1879) II² 828.

[13] Cf. *supra*, p. 6 at n. 10. A. Busse, *Die neoplatonischen Ausleger der Isagoge des Porphyrius* (*Wissenschaftliche Beilage zum Programm des Friedrichs-Gymnasiums zu Berlin, Ostern 1892* [Berlin 1892]) 3: 'Zwar fehlt es im Kommentar nicht an Spuren christlicher Anschauung, aber diese Stellen sind sämtlich auf Kosten der Abschreiber zu setzen, wie denn überhaupt die Schrift starke Erweiterungen erfahren hat.'

[14] Busse *loc. cit.*: 'Als Lebenszeit des Philosophen dürfen wir auf Grund der doppelten Beziehung, auf seinen Lehrer Proclus, welcher 485 starb, und auf seine Schüler Damascius und Simplicius, welche 529 nach Persien auswanderten, und Olympiodor, . . . die zweite Hälfte des fünften und den Anfang des sechsten Jahrhunderts festsetzen . . . Die Geburt unseres Philosophen dürfte in die Jahre 457 bis 474 fallen.' Brandt, CSEL 48, xxii.

[15] PWK II, v, 203–213 (Praechter): 'Simplicius ist neben Alexander v. Aphrodisias der schätzenwerteste unter den erhaltenen philosophischen Kommentatoren des Altertums';

Aristotle, he tells us that he depended much on Iamblichus. The calibre of his work is very highly regarded and his glory adds to that of his master, Ammonius. A second pupil of Ammonius is Olympiodorus who died in 564.[16] He wrote commentaries on Plato and Aristotle and was probably not a Christian. In his commentaries on the Categories and on the *Isagoge*, the latter of which is lost, he leans heavily on Ammonius; this work was used by his pupils, David and Elias. Olympiodorus wrote works on Plato's *Alcibiades*, *Gorgias*, *Phaedo* and *Philebus*, and also *In Aristotelis Meteora*. Asclepius of Tralles was also a pupil of Ammonius and he lived somewhat longer than Simplicius, dying 560/570.[17] We possess his commentary on the Metaphysics of Aristotle. He was also acquainted with the works of Alexander Aphrodisias. Two of the pupils of Olympiodorus were particularly important for our purpose, the first of them being David the Armenian,[18] a Christian neoplatonist. His date is uncertain, but he appears to have lived in the second half of the sixth century. He was born in Hark, Armenia and his works though written in Greek were later translated into Armenian. His commentary on the *Isagoge* is extant along with an introduction to philosophy. Critics have made much of the diffuseness of his work, and his love for schematic treatment of any topic that arises will be noted later. Busse is of the opinion that the works we possess are not from the hand of David, but were compiled by his pupils.[19]

Closely allied to the work of David was that of his fellow student Elias, who flourished in the middle of the sixth century,[20] and became a Christian late in

---

cf. Simplicii *In Aristotelis Categorias Commentarium* (ed. C. Kalbfleisch, ALRB VIII, Berlin 1907). Christ–Schmid–Stählin II, 1063: 'S. nimmt ohne Vorbehalt alle Lehren der Schulüberlieferung an und hat, anders als Proklos, nur das Bestreben, überall nachzuweisen, dass Aristoteles mit Platon in voller Harmonie stehe.' This is interesting in view of the ambition of Boethius mentioned above. Cf. C. Prantl, *Geschichte der Logik im Abendlande* (Leipzig 1927), I, 643; Zeller, *op. cit.* II², 829.

[16] PWK XVIII, 1, 207–227 (R. Beutler). Olympiodori *Prolegomena et in Categorias Commentarium* (ed. A. Busse, ALRB XII, i, Berlin, 1902) and Olympiodori *In Aristototelis Meteora Commentaria* (ed. W. Stüve, ALRB XII, ii, Berlin 1900); Olympiodori philosophi *In Platonis Gorgiam Commentaria* (ed. W. Norvin, Leipzig 1936). On these commentators, cf. 'Conspectus Commentatorum Graecorum,' in: Porphyrii *Isagoge et in Aristotelis Categorias Commentarium* (A. Busse, ALRB IV i, xxxiv-l).

[17] PWK II, 1697–98 (Freudenthal); Zeller, V, 843, 1; Asclepii *In Aristotelis Metaphysicorum Libros A–Z Commentaria* (ed. M. Hayduck, ALRB VI, ii, Berlin 1888).

[18] PWK IV, 2232 (Kroll); K. Krumbacher, *Geschichte der Byzantinischen Literatur* (München 1897) 432; Busse, *Ausleger* 13–20; C. F. Neumann, *Mémoire sur la vie et les ouvrages de David, philosophe Arménien* (Paris 1829): 'L'ouvrage qui donne véritablement un rang à David parmi les plus grands philosophes et les plus savans hommes de son siècle, est celui qui est intitulé *Fondemens de la Philosophie*' (cited from *Ausleger* 18). *Davidis Prolegomena et in Porphyrii Isagogen Commentarium* (ed. A. Busse, ALRB XVIII, ii, Berlin 1904).

[19] *Ausleger* 14; Prantl, *op. cit.* I, 642: '. . . da dort auch noch Ammonius erwähnt wird, so muss David nicht zu weit in das 5. Jahrh. zurück, sondern mehr in die erste Hälfte des 6. gesetzt werden.'

[20] Krumbacher, *op. cit.* 432; Eliae *In Porphyrii Isagogen et Aristotelis Categorias Commentaria* (ed. A. Busse, ALRB XVIII, i, Berlin 1900).

life. It seems probable that he wrote his commentaries with those of David at his side. We have works on the *Isagoge* and on the Categories from his pen. Another of the Christians among these commentators is John Philoponus the Grammarian who became Bishop of Alexandria and had been a pupil of Ammonius and of the grammarian, Romanus.[21] His literary activity was concerned with Grammar, Philosophy and Theology. In this latter field he seems to have fallen into serious error as he was condemned as a Tritheist. He wrote on the Categories and on the *Analytica Priora*.

The technique of introduction to a commentary, which we have seen in the grammarians called an *accessus* and among the jurists a *materia*, was among the philosophers referred to as τὰ εἰωθότα κεφάλαια[22] and occasionally as διδασκαλικά, the term which was adopted by Boethius. Nowhere more than among the philosophers do we get the impression that we are dealing with a rigidly prescribed program, a traditional formula obligatory on all philosophical commentators. Thus, Ammonius: δεῖ δὲ ἡμᾶς εἰπεῖν καὶ τὰ πρὸς τῶν φιλοσόφων οὕτω προσαγορευόμενα προλεγόμενα ἤτοι προτεχνολογούμενα ἐπὶ παντὸς βιβλίου.[23] Again he says in another work: Ἑπόμενον δὲ ἔννατόν ἐστι ζητῆσαι πόσα καὶ ποῖα δεῖ προλαμβάνεσθαι τῆς ἐξηγήσεως παντός Ἀριστοτελικοῦ βιβλίου.[24] And, Olympiodorus: διὰ μὲν οὖν τὰς κατηγορίας, τοῦτ' ἐστι τὸ σύγγραμμα, ζητήσωμεν ἔξ τινα, πάντοτε εἰωθότα πάντος βιβλίου προλέγεσθαι.[25]

The second striking detail in the method of the philosophers is that they are not satisfied merely to announce the items they will include in their introductory discussion, but they give reasons why it is judged fitting and necessary to handle precisely those points. Where in the other commentators one or other point, being superfluous,[26] would be omitted without mention, the philosophers include them all in their preliminary treatment and then give reasons why the specific treatment of some of them would be unnecessary. Hence it is clear that they are more rigidly bound to follow the customary formula. Thirdly, we find that the discussion of each of the points of the introduction has among

[21] PWK IX, ii, 1764–1795 (Kroll); Krumbacher *op. cit.* 581; Prantl, *op. cit.* I, 643; Kroll: 'zweifellos einer der produktivisten, vielseitigsten und gelehrtesten seiner Zeit.' Philoponi *In Aristotelis Categorias Commentarium* (ed. A. Busse, ALRB XIII, i, Berlin 1898); *In Analytica priora* (ed. M. Wallies, ALRB XIII, ii, Berlin 1905); *In Aristotelis Analytica posteriora Commentaria* (ed. M. Wallies, ALRB XIII, iii, Berlin 1909).

[22] Cf. David, *Isagoge* (ALRB XVIII, ii) 83, 8 and Elias, *In Isagogen* (ALRB XVIII, i) 35, 5 and 127, 5. Ammon. *De Interp.* (ALRB IV, v) 1, 13.

[23] Ammonius, *In Isagogen* 21, 6–8.

[24] Ammonius, *In Categorias* 7, 15–16.

[25] Olympiodorus, *In Categorias* 1, 10–12.

[26] Cf. David, *In Isagogen* 80–81: Οὐ περιττὸν δέ τι ποιοῦντες ταῦτα ζητοῦσιν, ἀλλὰ βουλόμενοι προθυμοτέρους τοὺς ἀναγινώσκοντας ἀπεργάσασθαι· καὶ γὰρ τὸν σκοπὸν ζητοῦσιν, ἐπειδὴ ὁ σκοπὸς ἐν συντόμῳ περιέχει πάντα τὰ ἐν τῷ λόγῳ λεγόμενα καὶ ἕξιν τινὰ ἐν τῷ ἀναγινώσκοντι τίθησι. ὁ γὰρ τὸν σκοπὸν ἀγνοῶν ὀκνηρότερος ἐπὶ τὸ σύγγραμμα ἔρχεται, ὥσπερ οἱ μακρὰν ὁδὸν ἀπιόντες καὶ ἀγνοοῦντες ποῦ ἀπέρχονται. καὶ ἁπλῶς εἰπεῖν ὁ τὸν σκοπὸν ἀγνοῶν ἔοικε τυφλῷ βαδίζοντι καὶ πολλὰ μοχθοῦντι· . . . εὐλόγως δὲ καὶ τὸ χρήσιμον ζητοῦσιν, ἐπειδὴ ἐὰν γινώσκῃ ἕκαστος τὸ ἐκ τοῦ συγγράμματος ἀναφυόμενον χρήσιμον, προθυμότερον ἀναγινώσκει τὸ σύγγραμμα. Cf. Ammonius, *In Categorias* 13, 25 and *ibid.* 7, 20.

these commentators a much wider scope, and the size of their introductions—far greater than in the other fields we have examined—is some indication of the importance which they attached to this part of their work. Fourth, and most important of all, the items that we are accustomed to find in this technique in other fields are, in the commentators on Aristotle, merely a part of a larger framework, consisting of ten questions that, apparently, had to be answered in every commentary on a work of Aristotle.[27] The last of these questions includes the items that we have been discussing. The importance of this fact should not be overlooked since here we find the formula that was adopted by later commentators as an integral part of this larger *schema*, into which it fits very naturally. It is difficult to escape the conclusion that here we have a source from which the practice came into being. This point will be taken up again, later, when we have before us the materials of the discussion.[28]

The points considered in this general introduction to Aristotle are the following:

1. The number and kinds of names given to philosophical sects?
2. Division of the works of Aristotle?
3. With what works must we begin the study of Aristotle?
4. What is the purpose of the philosophy of Aristotle?
5. What will help us to attain this purpose?
6. What is the character of the works of Aristotle?
7. Why did Aristotle choose to be obscure in his exposition?
8. What should be the proper attitude of a commentator on Aristotle?
9. What attitude should the reader of Aristotle adopt?
10. *How many items, and what kind of items, should be considered in the introductions to each work of Aristotle, and for what reasons?*[29]

It will be immediately evident that the elaboration of answers to all of these questions would have given rise to a great deal of speculation on the works of Aristotle, and it could not help but have sharpened the focus of the ideas of the commentators and their students. It is to be noted that these ten questions are not found, at least in the light of the extant works of these men, in commentaries on Porphyry or on any other philosopher than Aristotle. This would suggest that something in Aristotle himself might have been a motivating force in the construction of this *schema*, and this possibility will be mentioned later.

[27] All of the commentators who use these ten points, Ammonius, Olympiodorus, Elias, Simplicius and John Philoponus, stress the fact that this must be done in the introduction to every work of Aristotle; cf. their introductions, *opp. citt.*

[28] Cf. *infra*, pp. 48–49.

[29] Simplicius, *In Categorias* (ALRB VIII, 3, 18–29): Ἐπεὶ δὲ πρώτῳ τῶν Ἀριστοτέλους τῷ τῶν κατηγοριῶν ἐντυγχάνομεν βιβλίῳ, μία δὲ τῶν κατὰ φιλοσοφίαν αἱρέσεών ἐστιν ἡ Ἀριστοτέλους περιπατητικὴ καλουμένη, ῥητέον πρῶτον, κατὰ πόσους καὶ ποίους τρόπους τὰς ὀνομασίας ἔσχον αἱ κατὰ φιλοσοφίαν αἱρέσεις, δεύτερον, τίς ἡ διαίρεσις τῶν Ἀριστοτελικῶν συγγραμμάτων, ἵνα καὶ τὸ προκείμενον ὅπου χοροῦ τάξωμεν γένηται δῆλον, τρίτον, πόθεν ἀρκτέον τῶν Ἀριστοτέλους συγγραμμάτων, τέταρτον, τί τὸ τέλος ἐστὶν τῆς Ἀριστοτέλους φιλοσοφίας, πέμπτον, τίνα τὰ ἄγοντα ἡμᾶς πρὸς τὸ τέλος, ἕκτον, τί τὸ εἶδος τῶν Ἀριστοτελικῶν συγγραμμάτων, ἕβδομον, διὰ τί τὴν ἀσάφειαν ἐπετήδευσεν ὁ φιλόσοφος, ὄγδοον, ποῖον δεῖ τὸν ἐξηγητὴν εἶναι τῶν τοιούτων λόγων, ἔνατον, ποῖον δεῖ τὸν ἀκροατὴν παραλαμβάνεσθαι, δέκατον, πόσα δεῖ προλαμβάνειν ἑκάστης Ἀριστοτελικῆς πραγματείας κεφάλαια καὶ ποῖα καὶ διὰ ποίαν αἰτίαν.

The answers to these questions of the commentators present many very interesting ideas, which, however, are not germane to our purpose. The answer to the last of these questions takes the form of διδασκαλικά and the suggested justification of most of them is to be noted.

Δέκατον λοιπὸν ἦν τῶν προτεθέντων, πόσα χρὴ κεφάλαια καὶ τίνα τῶν Ἀριστοτέλους πραγματειῶν προδιαρθροῦσθαι. καὶ ἔστι ταῦτα ὁ σκοπός, τὸ χρήσιμον, ἡ τῆς ἐπιγραφῆς αἰτία, ἡ τάξις τῆς ἀναγνώσεως, εἰ γνήσιον τοῦ φιλοσόφου τὸ βιβλίον, ἡ εἰς τὰ κεφάλαια διαίρεσις· οὐκ ἄτοπον δὲ ἴσως ζητεῖν καὶ ὑπὸ ποῖον μέρος αὐτοῦ τῆς φιλοσοφίας ἀνάγεται. ὁ μὲν γὰρ σκοπὸς ὀρθῶς γνωσθεὶς ὁρίζει καὶ κατευθύνει τὴν διάνοιαν ἡμῶν, ἵνα μὴ ἐπ᾽ ἄλλα καὶ ἄλλα φερώμεθα μάτην, ἀλλὰ πρὸς αὐτὸν ἅπαντα ἀναφέρωμεν. τὸ δὲ χρήσιμον προφανὲν συντονωτέρους ἡμᾶς καὶ προθυμοτέρους ἐργάζεται. ἡ δὲ αἰτία τῆς ἐπιγραφῆς, ὅταν σαφὴς οὖσα τυγχάνῃ, οὐκ ἐνοχλεῖ, καὶ προσαφηνισθεῖσα δὲ βεβαιοῖ τὸν σκοπόν. καὶ τὸ γνήσιον δέ, ὅπερ, ὡς ἐμοὶ δοκεῖ, πρὸ πάντων ἔδει τῶν ἄλλων βασανίζεσθαι, ἀναγκαίως προλαμβάνεται· . . . ἡ δὲ εἰς τὰ κεφάλαια τῶν βιβλίων διαίρεσις οἷον κατ᾽ ἄρθρα τέμνουσα μιμεῖται τὴν ἀνατομικὴν παρὰ τοῖς ἰατροῖς θεωρίαν· ὡς γὰρ ἐκείνη τὴν εἰς τὸ ὅλον τείνουσαν χρείαν ἑκάστου τῶν μορίων διὰ τῆς ἀνατομῆς εὑρίσκει καὶ γνῶσιν ἀκριβεστέραν τοῦ συνθέτου παρέχεται παραγυμνώσασα τὰ ἁπλᾶ, οὕτως καὶ αὕτη διελοῦσα τὸ ὅλον ὑπ᾽ ὄψιν μᾶλλον ἄγει, καὶ τὴν ἑκάστου παρίστησιν χρείαν πρὸς τὸν ὅλον σκοπόν. καὶ τὸ δεῖξαι δὲ ὑπὸ ποῖον ἀνάγεται μέρος τὴν τοῦ μέρους πρὸς τὸ ὅλον παρέχεται σύνταξιν. ἰστέον δέ, ὅτι οὐκ ἀεὶ ταῦτα πάντα δεῖται διαρθρώσεως· πολλάκις γὰρ τὸ χρήσιμον τῷ σκοπῷ συναναφαίνεται καὶ ἡ ἐπιγραφὴ παντὶ δήλη καθέστηκεν, ὡς ἡ Περὶ Ψυχῆς, καὶ τὸ γνήσιον οὐκ ἐπὶ πάντων δεῖται κατασκευῆς, ἀλλ᾽ ἐφ᾽ ὧν ἔστιν τις ὅλως ἀντιλογίας ἀφορμή.[30]

It will readily be seen that these are the same points which we saw mentioned by Boethius, with the exception of one, which is here added, namely: ἡ εἰς τὰ κεφάλαια διαίρεσις τοῦ βιβλίου, that is, the sections into which Aristotle has divided this particular book. As will be seen from the accompanying chart, David and Elias make one further addition, ὁ τρόπος διδασκαλικός,[31] that is, the manner of instruction, which are said to be four, according to Aristotle, διαιρετικός, ὁριστικός, ἀποδεικτικός, ἀναλυτικός,[32] and according to David, all four are here used by Porphyry. What Boethius called ordo and is here referred to as ἡ τάξις τῆς ἀναγνώσεως, is distinct from the division of this work, in that it treats of the logical place for this work, in the whole Aristotelian system. Olympiodorus once gives auctor: ὁ συγγραφεύς. In place of ἡ διαίρεσις εἰς τὰ κεφάλαια, he uses ἡ διασκευὴ τοῦ βιβλίου.[33]

The accompanying chart of the use of this practice among the philosophers will be seen to include brief mention of a fragmentary use of it, in Proclus, Porphyrius, and Alexander Aphrodisias. The last of these is the most important of the Aristotelian commentators. He was a teacher of philosophy at Athens between 198 and 210, and the influence of his speculative mind on later Greek commentators and on the Arabs was extraordinarily wide. He was

[30] Simplicius, *In Categorias* 8, 28–9, 3.
[31] David, *In Isagogen* 83, 93; Elias, *In Isagogen* 39, and *In Categorias* 129.
[32] Aristotle, *Analytica Priora* 43b 1–25.
[33] Olympiodorus, *In Categorias* 1, 13.

known as ὁ ἐξηγήτης and there are extant commentaries of his on the *Analytica Priora I* and *Topica*. No longer extant are his commentaries on the Categories, *De interpretatione*, *Analytica Priora II* and *Analytica Posteriora*.[34] It was his work on the *De anima* that had such widespread influence on the Arabs and seems to have been the source of their doctrine of a separate *intellectus agens* which met with such opposition in the twelfth century.[35] His influence was strong on all of the commentators of the sixth century, and Ammonius and

USE OF THE διδασκαλικά BY THE PHILOSOPHERS

	Ammon.[a]	Simpl.[b]	Asclep.[c]	Olymp.[d]	Philop.[e]	David[f]	Elias[g]	Al. Aphr.[h]	Proc.[i]	Porph.[j]
ὁ σκοπός	1	1	1	1	1	1	1	1	1	2
τὸ χρήσιμον	2	2	2	2	2	2	2	2	—	3
τὸ γνήσιον	3	5	5[k]	5[l]	6	3	5	—	—	—
ἡ τάξις	4	4	3	3	4	6	3	—	—	—
ἡ ἐπιγραφή	5	3	4	4	3	4	4	—	—	1
ἡ διαίρεσις	6	6	—	6	5	5	6	—	—	—
ὑπὸ ποῖον μέρος	7	7	—	7	—	8	8	—	—	—
ὁ διδασκαλικὸς τρόπος	—	—	—	—	—	7	7	—	—	—
πόθεν ἦλθεν εἰς ἔννοιαν	—	—	6	—	—	—	—	—	—	—
τὸ εἶδος τῶν λόγων	—	—	—	—	—	—	—	—	2	—
ἡ ὕλη	—	—	—	—	—	—	—	—	3	—

a) Ammonius, *In Isagogen*; *In Categorias* and *De interp.* omit ποῖον μέρος, *Analytica Priora* omits ἡ διαίρεσις.   b) Simplicius, *In Categorias*.   c) Asclepius, *In Metaphysica*.   d) Olympiodorus, *In Categorias*; *In Meteora* omits ποῖον μέρος. *In Platonis Gorgiam* has ἡ δραματικὴ διασκευή, σκοπός, διαίρεσις, πρόσωπα τοῦ διαλόγου.   e) Philoponus, *In Categorias*; *Analytica priora* adds ποῖον μέρος.   f) David, *In Isagogen*.   g) Elias, *In Isagogen*; *In Categorias* omits ποῖον μέρος.   h) Alex. Aphrodisias, *In Analytica priora*; *In Sophisticis Elenchis* gives ὁ σκοπός, ἡ τάξις and ὅτου χάριν.   i) Proclus, *In Platonis Rem Publicam*.   j) Porphyrius, *In Categorias*.   k) Asclepius here has περὶ τοῦ μεγάλου Α καὶ περὶ μικροῦ Α.   l) Olympiodorus here has ὁ συγγραφεύς.

Simplicius are high in their praise of him.[36] Boethius seems to have known only his work on the *De interpretatione*, which he cites continually in his own

[34] Alexandri *In Aristotelis Analyticorum Priorum Librum I Commentarium* (ed. M. Wallies, ALRB II, i, Berlin 1883) and Alexandri *Quod fertur in Aristotelis Sophisticos Elenchos Commentarium* (ed. M. Wallies, ALRB II, iii, Berlin 1898); Prantl, *op. cit.* I, 621; 'Sein Reichtum an historischem Material machte ihn uns schon oben bei den Untersuchungen über die Peripatetiker und Stoiker oft zur einzigen Quelle, und in dieser Beziehung könnten wir alle übrigen Commentatoren, mit Ausnahme höchstens des Simplicius, sehr leicht vermissen, wenn die Schriften Alexanders erhalten wären.' Cf. PWK I, 1453–55 (Gercke); Christ–Schmid–Stählin II, 489.

[35] E. Gilson, 'Les sources gréco-arabes de l'augustinisme avicennisant', *Archives d'histoire doctrinale et littéraire du moyen âge* 4 (Paris 1929) 5–149.

[36] The copious references to Alexander in the editions of the sixth-century commentators bear eloquent testimony to this popularity.

commentary.[37] Porphyrius (233–304) is known particularly for his famous *Isagoge* and for εἰς τὰς 'Αριστοτέλους κατηγορίας κατὰ πεῦσιν καὶ ἀπόκρισιν.[38] The reverence with which he is cited by the commentators of the sixth century and the diligence with which they commented on his works is sufficient indication of his influence. Proclus was a teacher of Ammonius as has been mentioned above and hence it is likely that he had some influence on the commentatorial method of his pupil. Elias, in the beginning of his commentary on the Categories seems to imply that the use of the ten questions at the outset of a commentary on a work of Aristotle was practiced by Proclus.[39] He does not say that Proclus invented it. In any case it will be seen that these three commentators have some hint of the technique that was later developed so minutely.

Of particular significance as a manifestation of an advance in critical scholarship is the point as to the authenticity of the work in question. Thus, Olympiodorus in his introduction to the Categories felt no need to prove that Aristotle had written the work, since this was admitted by all. But he did go into the general question as to how books came to be falsely attributed to famous writers. This happens, he says, through deliberate falsification owing to the rivalry of kings who wish to enhance the reputation of their libraries, or through the partiality of pupils, who wish their particular master to be considered the author of a notable work. Also, a false attribution may arise through similarity of name of an author, or a work, or through a misunderstanding of a reference to a book by a later author. Olympiodorus promised to discuss the criteria by which spurious and authentic works might be distinguished, but unfortunately, he does not seem to have followed out his intention.[40]

The question ὑπό ποῖον μέρος τῆς φιλοσοφίας was also of great importance for these philosophers and they are most detailed in their exposition of the point.[41] We have already seen that the grammarians and the jurists included *pars philosophiae* in their introductions, rather mechanically declaring their work to come under the heading of Ethics. Among the philosophers, however, the matter was of real significance because of a long-standing controversy and it affected their attitude toward the study of Logic in general. The Stoics had held that Logic was really a part of philosophy, the Peripatetics that it was merely an

---

[37] *Op. cit. (supra*, p. 29 n. 1) II, 505; Théry, *op. cit. (supra*, p. 30 n. 2) 17 believes that Boethius knew only this work of Alexander.

[38] Porphyrii *Isagoge et in Aristotelis Categorias Commentarium* (ed. A. Busse, ALRB IV, i, Berlin 1887); Prantl I, 626–638; Christ–Schmid–Stählin II,2, 678; Zeller, *Die Philosophie der Griechen* III², 631–677.

[39] Cf. Zeller, *op. cit.* 774–826; Prantl I, 641; Proclus, *In Platonis Rem Publicam* (ed. W. Kroll, Leipzig 1899, 2 vols.) and *In Platonis Timaeum* (ed. E. Diehl, Leipzig 1903); Elias, *In Categ.* 107, 24–26: ταῦτα πάντα τοῦ Πρόκλου λέγοντος δεῖν προλαμβάνειν ἀρχομένους τῶν 'Αριστοτελικῶν συνταγμάτων ἐν τῇ συναναγνώσει. . . .

[40] It has been deemed advisable in view of the value of this item for an estimate of the scholarly stature of these commentators to give, on this point of τὸ γνήσιον, and on the following note ὑπὸ ποῖον μέρος τῆς φιλοσοφίας ἀνάγεται a rather large portion of their text. These will be found in *Excursus B, infra*, pp. 40–41.

[41] Cf. *Excursus B, infra*, pp. 41–42; Zeller II², 182.

instrument, and Plato, that it was both a part and an instrument, under different aspects. For the most part they are at one with Aristotle on this point, but all who mention it are at pains to outline the divergent views that had been held. In the other authors, then, the *pars philosophiae* is merely a survival of a stereotyped technique and of little significance; here, it has real meaning and this fact is one which leads the writer to believe that the *schema* had its origin among the philosophers, and was taken over from them by students of the other fields of medieval science. On this and many other points of this technique, the philosophers appear to be on more solid ground. Nowhere does the *schema* seem to be more at home than among them.

As an illustration of the attitude of mind which could very possibly have impelled the philosophers to invent such an elaborate *schema* there should be mentioned the work of David, προλεγόμενα τῆς φιλοσοφίας.[42] This introductory treatise purports to give the necessary information for one entering upon such a course and it is an extraordinarily complex, yet clear schematic arrangement of what he had to say. He opens with the mention of the four forms of inquiry outlined by Aristotle, εἰ ἔστι, τί ἐστι, ὁποῖόν τι ἐστι, διὰ τί ἐστι,[43] and proceeds to explain each point with almost countless subdivisions and parts. In treating the first point, as to the existence of philosophy, he mentions four questions.[44] On the second, the bulk of the treatise, as to what philosophy is, he speaks of the limits and scope of philosophy as a unit giving nine questions under ὅρος, nine more under ὁρισμός; of this latter group, he gives six subdivisions of the last two. He then goes on to the kinds of knowledge, four, and the instruments used by philosophy, five. Then as to the divisions of philosophy, he gives the views of Plato and Aristotle, and five divisions of speculative philosophy and eight different means of distinguishing the various parts. The six classic definitions of philosophy are given and reasons mentioned why there are six, no more and no less.[45] The last two parts of his treatise are equally divided and subdivided in much the same fashion as in the former. This is doubtless the *schematismus* to which Prantl objected so strenuously. Whether it be valuable or not as a contribution to philosophical thought, the elaborate structure of the work is a striking indication of an attitude of mind, a point of view which would have delighted in the accurate and detailed analysis of his subject, such as we have seen manifested by David and his contemporaries in the ten questions and in the seven or eight items of the *schema* that we have been studying. This is admittedly merely an indication and is not to be considered as proof of the origin of the *schema*. But, as contributory evidence it is not to be despised.

EXCURSUS A

Ammonius In Isagogen

Since we have made use of the items of the technique of the *accessus* as found in the commentary of Ammonius on the *Isagoge*, it is imperative here that we treat of the ques-

---

[42] Cf. David, προλεγόμενα τῆς φιλοσοφίας 1–79.

[43] Aristotle, *Analytica posteriora*, B 89b 2.

[44] David, *loc. cit.* 1–9.

[45] *Ibid.* 9–76.

tion that was raised by Busse in his edition of the commentary and in his *Ausleger*. In the latter work, Busse expounds his view that the very portion of the *prooemium* which contains the points we are interested in, was not written by Ammonius but was inserted later, perhaps from the works of Philoponus or Olympiodorus. He bases this opinion on his analysis of the *prooemium* which leads him to believe that we have a double introduction to the *Isagoge*, and therefore this latter portion is superfluous and spurious. It is proper then that this opinion of Busse, which seems to me to be false, should be explained at some length. His critical note *ad loc.* reads as follows:

5. Εἰς πόσα—ὡς ἐν ἐτέρῳ δείξομεν (p. 23–24). Nescio an ab Ammonio aliena sunt; etenim alteram praebent huius libri praefationem, qua ea quae Ammonius inde a verbis (p. 16, 17) Ἐμάθομεν τοίνυν τί ἐστι φιλοσοφία καὶ ποῖα αὐτῆς τὰ μέρη, propria explicandi ratione praefatus est, ratione in scholis trita, ut David et Elias ostendunt, repetuntur atque amplificantur.

In his *Ausleger*, in commenting on the charge of *schematismus* levelled at Ammonius by Prantl, he remarks:

Dies tritt besonders greifbar bei der Einleitung zur Isagoge hervor, welche in der heutigen Überlieferung doppelt vorliegt; nur der erste (p. 17, 1–20, 24) kann als echt gelten, die zweite (p. 21, 5–23, 24) hat sich wahrscheinlich aus dem Kommentar eines Schülers, des Philoponus oder Olympiodorus hier eingeschlichen . . . [Note 8] Dem erläuternden Kommentar werden zwei Einleitungen vorausgeschickt, die erste (prolegomenon philosophiae) enthält die allgemeine Einführung in die Philosophie durch Angabe der Definitionen und Einteilungen derselben, die zweite (prolegomena Isagoges) giebt über das vorliegende Buch die nötigen Bemerkungen. Ammonius stellt in diesem Abschnitt, soweit er echt ist, die Ableitung der Kategorien dar und begnügt sich Zweck und Titel der Isagoge zu bezeichnen. In der eingeschobenen Partie dagegen, welche mit dem Worten εἰς πόσα μὲν οὖν καὶ διαιρεῖται τῆς φιλοσοφίας ἕκαστον μέρος anhebt, als ob die Auseinandersetzung p. 17, 1–20, 24 gar nicht vorhanden wäre, werden in der schematischen Weise des David und Elias sieben Hauptpunkte der Betrachtung hervorgehoben und der Reihe nach durchgenommen. Wenn wir diesen Abschnitt streichen, so fällt damit freilich auch die Erzählung von dem Ursprunge der Isagoge. . . .

As appears from these citations, Busse divides the *prooemium* into two sections:
a) Prolegomenon philosophiae, p. 1, 5–p. 16, 17
b) Prolegomenon Isagoges, p. 16, 17–p. 20, 24,
considering the remaining section as spurious and unnecessary since p. 21, 5–p. 23, 24, is merely a repetition of the preceding. As a matter of fact, the prooemium really has three sections:
a) Prolegomenon philosophiae, p. 1, 5–p. 16, 17
b) Prolegomenon Aristotelis Categoriarum, p. 16, 17–p. 20, 14
c) Prolegomenon Isagoges, p. 20, 15–p. 23, 24.
Thus we see that the *prooemium* opened with these words : Μέλλοντας ἡμᾶς ἄρχεσθαι φιλοσόφων λόγων ἀναγκαῖόν ἐστι μαθεῖν τί ποτέ ἐστι φιλοσοφία. Thence followed the discussion of the various definitions of philosophy such as we have found in the other commentators, the divisions of philosophy and various examples, all of which extends to p. 16, 17, and he concludes with these words : Ἐμάθομεν τοίνυν τί ἐστι φιλοσοφία καὶ ποῖα αὐτῆς τὰ μέρη. Ammonius then continues as follows:

τοσαῦτα μὲν κοινῶς ὑπὲρ φιλοσοφίας εἰρήσθω. ἰδίᾳ δὲ περὶ τοῦ προκειμένου βιβλίου λέγομεν ταῦτα. Εἴρηται ὅτι φιλοσοφία γνῶσις τῶν ὄντων ᾖ ὄντα ἐστίν. ἐζήτησαν οὖν οἱ φιλόσοφοι, τίνα ἂν τρόπον γένοιντο τῶν ὄντων ἐπιστήμονες.

As he says: So much for philosophy in general; now to come to specific items, he mentions περὶ τοῦ προκειμένου βιβλίου and proceeds to discuss not the *Isagoge* of Porphyry (as Busse avers) to which this whole *prooemium* is prefixed, but rather *the Categories of Aristotle*, to which Porphyry had written his *Isagoge*, or introduction.   That it was Ammonius' intention to offer this preliminary explanation of the scope of the work of Aristotle, as a help to understanding the work of Porphyry, becomes clear when we read his summation and his concluding words, in which he tells us what he thinks he has done:

ἔσχον οὖν δέκα τοιαύτας κοινότητας·   οὐσίαν ποσὸν ποιὸν πρός τι ποῦ ποτὲ κεῖσθαι ἔχειν ποιεῖν πάσχειν.   ἕκαστον οὖν τῶν ὄντων πάντων ὑπὸ μίαν τούτων τελεῖ τῶν κοινοτήτων. ταύτας δὲ ἐκάλεσαν κατηγορίας ὡς κατά τινων τῶν ὑπ' αὐτὰς τελούντων ἀγορευομένας καὶ λεγομένας.   Περὶ τούτων οὖν τῶν δέκα κατηγοριῶν ὁ Ἀριστοτέλης ἔγραψεν βιβλίον καὶ ἐμνήσθη ἐν τῇ διδασκαλίᾳ φωνῶν τινων πέντε ἀγνώστων ἡμῖν οὐσῶν ἐν τῇ συνηθείᾳ γένους διαφορᾶς εἴδους ἰδίου καὶ συμβεβηκότος.   ὁ γοῦν φιλόσοφος Πορφύριος . . . ἔγραψε τουτὶ τὸ βιβλίον διδάσκων ἡμᾶς, τί σημαίνει ἑκάστη φωνή, ἵνα μαθόντες εὐχερέστερον δυνηθῶμεν παρακολουθεῖν τοῖς ὑπὸ τοῦ Ἀριστοτέλους λεγομένοις περὶ τῶν κατηγοριῶν.

In other words, the *prooemium* first discusses philosophy in general, κοινῶς ὑπὲρ φιλοσοφίας and then, the ten Categories of being, the content of Aristotle's *Categoriae*, περὶ τοῦ προκειμένου βιβλίου and finally, Porphyry's *Isagoge* τουτὶ τὸ βιβλίον.   Consequently, each of these three sections is a necessary part of his *prooemium* and there is no needless repetion, as charged by Busse.   It is this latter section that handles the seven points of the διδασκαλικά.   If Busse intends (as the trend of his argument seems to imply) that Ammonius did not know this technique, he must have forgotten that they are used by Ammonius in his commentary on the Categories (ed. Busse, ALRB IV, iv, p. 7, 15– p. 13, 30) and in that on *De Interpretatione* (ed. Busse, ALRB IV, v, p. 1, 3–p. 8, 28).

EXCURSUS B

Olympiodorus, *Prolegomena*, pp. 13,7–14,4; cf. *supra*, p. 37 n. 40.

Ἐνοθεύοντο τοίνυν τὰ βιβλία τὸ παλαιὸν κατὰ τρεῖς τρόπους·   ἢ διὰ φιλοτιμίαν τῶν βασιλέων, ἢ δι' εὔνοιαν τῶν μαθητῶν ἢ διὰ ὁμωνυμίαν.   καὶ δι' ὁμωνυμίαν τριχῶς· ἢ συγγράφεως ἢ συγγραμμάτων ἢ ὑπομνημάτων.   ἀλλ', εἰ δοκεῖ, μάθωμεν πῶς τὸ τῶν βασιλέων φιλότιμον αἴτιον ἦν τοῦ τὰς βίβλους νοθεύεσθαι.   ἰστέον τοίνυν ὅτι οἱ παλαιοὶ βασιλεῖς ἐρασταὶ ὄντες λόγων ἔσπευδον διὰ φιλοτιμίας συναγαγεῖν τὰ τῶν ἀρχαίων συγγράμματα.   οὕτως οὖν Ἰοβάτης ὁ τῆς Λιβύης βασιλεὺς ἐραστὴς ἐγένετο τῶν Πυθαγορικῶν συγγραμμάτων καὶ Πτολεμαῖος ὁ ἐπίκλην Φιλάδελφος τῶν Ἀριστοτελικῶν καὶ Πεισίστρατος ὁ τῶν Ἀθηναίων τύραννος τῶν Ὁμηρικῶν ⟨καὶ⟩ χρημάτων δωρεαῖς ἔσπευδον ταῦτα συναγαγεῖν.   πολλοὶ οὖν χρημάτων ὀρεγόμενοι ἔσπευδον ἢ συγγράψασθαι ἤγουν καὶ τὰ τυχόντα συναγαγεῖν καὶ ἐπιγράφειν τοῖς τῶν ἀρχαιοτέρων ὀνόμασι καὶ προσφέρειν καὶ καρποῦσθαι δωρεὰς διὰ τούτου μνηστευόμενοι.   καὶ συνέβαινεν, ὡς προείπομεν, νοθεύεσθαι τὰ βιβλία διὰ φιλοτιμίαν βασιλέων.

διὰ δὲ ὁμωνυμίαν συγγράφεων ἐνοθεύοντο ἔσθ' ὅτε τὰ βιβλία, διότι μὴ εἷς καὶ μόνος Ἀριστοτέλης ὁ Σταγειρίτης ἐγένετο, ἀλλὰ καὶ ὁ ἐπίκλην Μῦθος, ἀλλὰ δὴ καὶ ὁ καλούμενος Παιδοτρίβης.   δι' ὁμωνυμίαν δὲ συγγραμμάτων ἐνοθεύοντο τὰ βιβλία, διότι μὴ μόνος Ἀριστοτέλης ἔγραψε Κατηγορίας, ἀλλὰ καὶ Θεόφραστος καὶ Εὔδημος, οἱ τούτου μαθηταί. πολλάκις οὖν τις περιτυχὼν ταῖς Κατηγορίαις Θεοφράστου, εἰ τύχοι, ἐνόμισεν αὐτὰς εἶναι Ἀριστοτέλους. ἔσθ᾽ ὅτε δὲ οὐδὲ διὰ ὁμωνυμίαν συγγράφεων ἐνοθεύοντο τὰ βιβλία οὐδὲ διὰ ὁμωνυμίαν συγγραμμάτων, ἀλλὰ διὰ ὁμωνυμίαν ὑπομνημάτων, διότι πολλάκις ὑπόμνημά τις ἐποίησεν εἰς ὁμώνυμον πραγματείαν καὶ ἐνομίσθη ἄλλης εἶναι· ὥσπερ οὖν καὶ Θεόφραστος ἐποίησεν ὑπόμνημα εἰς τὰς οἰκείας Κατηγορίας, καὶ πολλάκις τις ἀποπλανᾶται ὅτι τῶν Ἀριστοτέλους ἐστὶ τὸ ὑπόμνημα. ἢ πολλάκις ἐντιγχάνων τις τῷ ὑπομνήματι Ἀλεξάνδρου τοῦ Ἀφροδισιέως εἰς τὰς Κατηγορίας ἐνόμιζεν αὐτὸ πάντως εἶναι τῶν Ἀριστοτέλους, λανθάνον ὅτι οὐ μόνον γέγραπται αὐτῷ εἰς τὰς Ἀριστοτέλους ἀλλὰ καὶ εἰς τὰς Θεοφράστου.

ἔστι δὲ ὅτε δι᾽ εὐγνωμοσύνην μαθητῶν πρὸς διδάσκαλον ἐνοθεύοντο τὰ βιβλία, ὥσπερ πάντα τὰ συγγράμματα τὰ ἐπιγεγραμμένα Πυθαγόρου. ὁ γὰρ Πυθαγόρας οὐκ ἀπέλειψεν οἰκεῖον σύγγραμμα, λέγων ὅτι οὐ δεῖ ἄψυχα καταλιμπάνειν συγγράμματα, ἐπειδὴ μὴ δύναται ὑπὲρ ἑαυτῶν ἀπολογεῖσθαι, ἀλλὰ δὴ καταλιμπάνειν ἔμψυχα συγγράμματα, τοῦτ᾽ ἔστι μαθητάς, οἵτινες καὶ ὑπὲρ ἑαυτῶν καὶ τῶν ἰδίων διδασκάλων δύνανται συμμαχεῖν. οἱ οὖν μαθηταὶ αὐτοῦ δι᾽ εὔνοιαν ποιήσαντες συγγράμματα ἐπέγραψαν τὸ ὄνομα Πυθαγόρου. καὶ διὰ ταύτην τὴν αἰτίαν νόθα εἰσὶ πάντα τὰ ἐξ ὀνόματος Πυθαγόρου προσφερόμενα συγγράμματα.

> Olympiodorus, *Prolegomena*, pp. 14,13–17,36; cf. *supra*, p. 37 n. 41.

Ἐπειδὴ τῶν προλεγομένων ἀρχόμενοι πρὸς τρία τινὰ τὴν διδασκαλίαν ὑπισχνούμεθα ποιήσασθαι, πρός τε πᾶσαν φιλοσοφίαν, τὴν ἐπιστήμην φημί, καὶ πρὸς τὴν μέθοδον, τοῦτ᾽ ἔστι τὴν λογικήν, καὶ πρὸς τὸ σύγγραμμα, τοῦτ᾽ ἔστι τὰς Κατηγορίας, φέρε διανύσαντες τὸ πρῶτον τῶν προτεθέντων ἡμῖν εἰς ἐξέτασιν ἐπὶ τὸ δεύτερον εὐτάκτως χωρήσωμεν, ἐπὶ τὴν μέθοδόν φημι, ζητοῦντες εἰ μέρος ἢ ὄργανον ἡ λογικὴ τῆς φιλοσοφίας. δεῖ τοίνυν εἰδέναι ὅτι διάφοροι δόξαι γεγόνασι περὶ ταύτης, τῶν μὲν Στωϊκῶν μέρος αὐτὴν εἶναι νομιζόντων, τῶν δὲ Περιπατητικῶν ὄργανον, τοῦ δὲ θείου Πλάτωνος μέρος ἅμα καὶ ὄργανον . .

Οἱ δὲ Στωϊκοὶ διὰ δύο ἐπιχειρημάτων τὴν ἰδίαν δόξαν ἐβούλοντο πιστώσασθαι, ὧν τὸ πρῶτον τοιαύτην ἔχει τὴν ἀγωγήν· πᾶν, ᾧ κέχρηταί τις ἢ τέχνη ἢ ἐπιστήμη, ἐὰν μὴ ᾖ ἑτέρας τέχνης ἢ ἐπιστήμης ⟨ἢ μέρος ἢ μόριον, αὐτῆς τῆς κεχρημένης⟩ ἢ μέρος ἢ μόριόν ἐστιν, οἷον ὡς ἐπὶ παραδειγμάτων· τῆς ἰατρικῆς τέχνης μέρος ἐστὶ τὸ διαιτητικόν, καὶ οὐδαμῶς ἑτέρας τέχνης ἢ ἐπιστήμης μέρος ἢ μόριόν ἐστι· τῆς ἰατρικῆς ἄρα τέχνης τὸ διαιτητικὸν μέρος ἐστί, καὶ αὕτη μόνη κέχρηται αὐτῷ. εἰ τοίνυν καὶ ἡ φιλοσοφία κέχρηται τῇ λογικῇ, ἑτέρα δὲ τέχνη ἢ ἐπιστήμη ταύτῃ οὐ κέχρηται, τῆς ἄρα φιλοσοφίας μέρος ἢ μόριον ἡ λογική. ἀλλὰ μὴν οὐ μόριον· μέρος ἄρα. καλῶς δὲ πρόσκειται τῷ λόγῳ τὸ ᾽ἐὰν μὴ ᾖ ἑτέρας τέχνης ἢ ἐπιστήμης᾽ διὰ τὴν ἀστρονομίαν. ἐκινδύνευεν γὰρ ἡ ἀστρονομία μέρος εἶναι τῆς κυβερνητικῆς, ἐπειδὴ κέχρηται αὐτῇ . . . ἀλλὰ μὴν καὶ τῇ λογικῇ οὐδεμία ἄλλη τις κέχρηται ἢ μόνη ἡ φιλοσοφία· ταύτης ἄρα τῆς χρωμένης μέρος ἢ μόριόν ἐστιν ἢ ὄργανον. ἀλλὰ μὴν οὐκ ἔστι μέρος ἢ μόριον ἡ λογική, ὡς δέδεικται· ὄργανον ἄρα ἐστί.

Οἱ δὲ τῶν Περιπατητικῶν λόγοι, τρεῖς ὄντες τὸν ἀριθμόν, τοιαύτην ἔχουσι τὴν ἀγωγήν, οἱ πρεσβεύοντες εἶναι ὄργανον τὴν λογικήν. καὶ ὁ μὲν πρῶτος αὐτῶν τοῦτον ἔχει τὸν τρόπον· ἐὰν ὦσι, φασί, δύο τέχναι καὶ κέχρηται ἡ ἑτέρα τῷ ἀποτελέσματι τῆς ἑτέρας, ἡ κεχρημένη κρείττων ἐστὶ τῆς ἀποτελεσάσης· οἷον ὡς ἔχει ἐπὶ χαλινοποιητικῆς καὶ ἱππικῆς· ἡ μὲν γὰρ χαλινοποιητικὴ χαλινὸν ἐποίησεν, ἡ δὲ ἱππικὴ τούτῳ ἐχρήσατο· οὐκοῦν ἄρα ἡ ἱππικὴ ὡς κεχρημένη τῷ ἀποτελέσματι τῆς χαλινοποιητικῆς κρείττων αὐτῆς ὑπάρχει. οὕτω καὶ ἡ κυβερνητικὴ ναυπηγικῆς ἐστι τιμιωτέρα, διότι τῷ πλοίῳ κέχρηται ἡ κυβερνητικὴ ἀποτελέσματι ὄντι τῆς ναυπηγικῆς. εἰ δὲ τοῦτο, ἐπειδὴ ἡ μὲν φιλοσοφία ποιεῖ τὴν λογικήν,

κέχρηνται δὲ αἱ ἄλλαι πᾶσαι τέχναι τῷ ἀποτελέσματι τῆς λογικῆς, οἷον ἰατρική, γραμμα-
τική, ῥητορική, καὶ ἁπλῶς εἰπεῖν αἱ παραπλήσιοι τέχναι, εὑρεθήσεται ἄρα ἡ φιλοσοφία
τῶν ἄλλων τεχνῶν τῶν κεχρημένων τῷ ταύτης προβλήματι, λέγω δὴ τῇ λογικῇ * * *
κρείττους τῆς φιλοσοφίας, ἐπεὶ ἀτοπίας πάσης ἐστὶν ἐπέκεινα· τίς γὰρ ἂν εἰς τοσαύτην
ἔλθοι ἀναίδειαν ὥστε τὴν μητέρα ὅλων τῶν τεχνῶν χείρονα ὀνομάσαι τῶν κατὰ μέρος
τεχνῶν; εἰ μὴ οὖν μέρος ἐστὶ διὰ τὸ ἄτοπον τοῦτο, ὄργανον ἄρα ἐστὶ τῆς φιλοσοφίας ἡ
λογική. καὶ ἐν τούτοις ἡ ἐπαγωγὴ τοῦ πρώτου ἐπιχειρήματος. δεύτερον ἐπιχείρημα
τοιαύτην ἔχον τὴν ἀγωγήν . . . . . τρίτον ἐπιχείρημα . . . . . καλῶς οὖν ἄρα συλλελόγισται
ἡμῖν ὅτι δι᾽ ἕτερον παραλαμβάνεται ἡ λογικὴ καὶ διὰ τοῦτο ὄργανον ἂν κληθείη. Ὅτι
δὲ εὖ λέγουσιν οἱ Περιπατητικοί, δείξωμεν καὶ ἡμεῖς δι᾽ ἑτέρων λόγων ὄργανον οὖσαν τὴν
λογικήν, ἐπισφραγίζοντες τοὺς ἤδη εἰρημένους λόγους ὡς ἀληθείας μετέχοντας. . . . .

Οἱ μὲν οὖν τῶν Περιπατητικῶν καὶ τῶν Στωικῶν λόγοι τοῦτον ἔχουσι τὸν τρόπον, ὁ
δὲ θεῖος Πλάτων καὶ μέρος αὐτὴν οἴεται εἶναι καὶ ὄργανον, ὅθεν οὐ δεῖται κατασκευῆς·
ἀμφότεροι γάρ, φησίν, ἐμοὶ νικᾶτε· διὰ τοῦτο γὰρ ἐπιχειρήματα εὐπορεῖτε ἑκάτεροι,
διότι ἡ λογικὴ τῆς φιλοσοφίας καὶ μέρος ἐστὶ καὶ ὄργανον, καὶ ἀληθεύετε, ἄνδρες, καὶ
μάχεσθε πρὸς ἀλλήλους μὴ μαχόμενοι· καὶ γὰρ μέρος ἐστὶ καὶ ὄργανον. καὶ μὴ νομίσητε
κατὰ τὸ αὐτὸ λέγειν με τοῦτο· κατ᾽ ἄλλο γὰρ καὶ ἄλλο μέρος ἐστὶ καὶ ὄργανον, ὡς
ἔστι ἐπὶ χειρὸς ἐξετάσαι τὸν λόγον καὶ τοῦ ξέστου· καὶ γὰρ ἡ χεὶρ καὶ μέρος ἐστὶ καὶ
ὄργανον, μέρος ἰὲν τοῦ ὅλου σώματος ὄργανον δὲ δόσεως καὶ λήψεως. ὁμοίως καὶ ὁ ξέστης
καὶ μέρος καὶ ὄργανόν ἐστι· ἐπειδὴ γὰρ διττὸς ὁ ξέστης, ὁ μὲν μετρῶν ὁ δὲ μετρούμενος,
δυνατὸν μέρος μὲν εἰπεῖν τὸν μετρούμενον ὄργανον δὲ τὸν μετροῦντα. . . οὕτω καὶ ἐπὶ τῆς
λογικῆς οὐδὲν ἄτοπον ἡμῖν συμβήσεται λέγουσιν αὐτὴν εἶναι καὶ μέρος καὶ ὄργανον·
ὄργανον μὲν ὅτε ἐν ψιλοῖς κανόσι θεωρεῖται, ὡς ὅτε εἴπω ὅτι ' ἐκ δύο καθόλου καταφατικῶν
καθόλου καταφατικὸν συνάγεται συμπέρασμα'. μέρος δὲ. . .ὅτε εἴπω ὅτι ' ἡ ψυχὴ αὐτοκίνητος,
τὸ αὐτοκίνητον ἀθάνατον, ἡ ψυχὴ ἄρα ἀθάνατος'.

IV. THE RHETORICIANS

Earlier in this paper mention has been made of the rhetoricians, Theon,
Hermogenes and Aphthonius. Przychocki, in connection with the origin of
the practice of the *accessus*, appeared to have satisfied himself that in the use of
the traditional rhetorical *circumstantiae*, namely: *Quis, quid, ubi, quibus auxiliis,
cur, quomodo, quàndo*, or their Greek equivalents, τὸ πρόσωπον, τὸ πρᾶγμα, ὁ
τόπος, ὁ χρόνος, ὁ τρόπος, ἡ αἰτία,[1] as found in these writers, he had found the
source from which this technique had come into the writings of the twelfth-
century commentators on classical literature. It will now be apparent that this
view is the result of a considerable over-simplification of the issues at stake.
These early rhetoricians do not manifest any acquaintance with the *schema*
that we have been studying, but their followers, the commentators on the works
of Hermogenes and Aphthonius, make constant use of this technique, in a form
strikingly similar to that used by the Aristotelian commentators. So much so
that it appears quite certain that the rhetorical commentators depend for their
knowledge of the practice on the philosophers we studied in the preceding

[1] Cf. *supra*, p. 13. Thus Theon, *Rhetores Graeci* (ed. L. Spengel [Leipzig 1854] II, 78).
Hermogenes lists ὁ τόπος, ὁ χρόνος, ὁ τρόπος, τὸ πρόσωπον, ἡ αἰτία, τὸ πρᾶγμα, ἡ ὕλη (*ibid.* II, 212);
and Aphthonius has: τὸ πρόσωπον, τὸ πρᾶγμα, ἡ αἰτία κτλ. (*ibid.* II, 49).

chapter. The rhetoricians, therefore, are not the source of the technique of the *accessus*, but rather, they were borrowers from the philosophers.

Our knowledge of Theon,[2] a Greek rhetorician who seems to have lived in the time of Quintilian, is very scanty, but there are extant some *progymnasmata* in which he discusses the six elements that should be accounted for in a proper narration. Hermogenes[3] lived in the latter half of the second century and, when a mere boy, enjoyed such a reputation for eloquence that the Emperor Marcus Aurelius went to hear him. When twenty-four years of age, Hermogenes suffered a complete loss of memory which incapacitated him for the rest of his long life. His works on rhetoric were: περὶ ἰδεῶν, περὶ εὑρέσεως, περὶ στάσεων, προγυμνάσματα, περὶ μεθόδου δεινότητος,[4] and they enjoyed an extraordinary popularity, being the subject of many commentaries. Aphthonius,[5] a pupil of Libanius, flourished in the second half of the fourth century, and he recast the *progymnasmata* of Hermogenes, and judging from the tone of his commentators, to some extent, outstripped his predecessor in reputation.

These commentators on the rhetoricians are for the most part anonymous although the excellent researches of Rabe have attempted to discover the identity of some of them.[6] They apparently wrote between the sixth and the eleventh centuries and while they are commenting on the works of the aforementioned rhetoricians, they clearly draw the ideas, in their introductions, from the *prooemia* of Ammonius, Olympiodorus, Simplicius, David and Elias.[7] Not only do they list all of the traditional items of the philosophers but they often draw illustrations from the *prooemia* to the commentaries on the *Isagoge* of Porphyry and in general, they show a thorough acquaintance with these writings.[8] Three points of distinction from the manner of the philosophers can be mentioned, but two of these are strikingly suggestive of an even deeper dependence on the philosophers. For instance, in place of ποῖον μέρος τῆς φιλοσοφίας

[2] Cf. PWK (K. Ziegler) II, 5, 2037–2054; J. E. Sandys, *A History of Classical Scholarship*, (Cambridge 1906) I, 318; C. S. Baldwin, *Medieval Rhetoric and Poetic* (New York 1928) 23.

[3] Christ–Schmid–Stählin VII, 2, 2, 729–736; PWK (Radermacher) VIII, 1, 865–877; Baldwin, *op. cit.* 23–39.

[4] Text in H. Rabe, *Rhetores Graeci* VI (Leipzig 1913) 213; 93; 28; 1; 414.

[5] PWK (Jülicher) I, 2797–2801; Sandys, *op. cit.* I, 319.

[6] H. Rabe, *Prolegomenon Sylloge*, in *Rhetores Graeci* XIV (Leipzig 1931). Rabe has here edited a collection of *prolegomena* to commentaries on the works of Aphthonius and Hermogenes. Thirty-four pieces are edited and of these, eleven show the *schema* in which we are interested. In the chart showing their use of this *schema*, which they occasionally call προθεωρία, Rabe's numbers will be found at the head of each column. Of these, ⌗8, ⌗9 and ⌗10 are *Prolegomena in Aphthonii Progymnasmata*; ⌗13, ⌗15, ⌗17 and ⌗20 are *Prolegomena in Hermogenis* περὶ στάσεων; ⌗27 is *in Hermogenis* περὶ εὑρέσεως, and ⌗28, ⌗32 and ⌗33 are *in Hermogenis* περὶ ἰδεῶν.

[7] Cf. Rabe *op. cit. passim*, where the *testimonia* are given above his *app. crit.*

[8] Cf. Rabe, *op. cit.* 73–74 and 134, 10, as follows: Ἀποροῦσι δέ τινες, πῶς ιδ' τῶν προγυμνασμάτων ὄντων ἕνα σκοπὸν οἴονται ἀποδοθῆναι ἁπάντων. καὶ λέγομεν ὅτι, ὥσπερ ε' φωνὰς τοῦ Πορφυρίου ἐν τῇ Εἰσαγωγῇ διδάσκοντος, γένος, διαφοράν, εἶδος, ἴδιον, συμβεβηκός, σκοπὸν ἕνα τοῦ τοιούτου βιβλίου οἱ ἐξηγούμενοι αὐτὸ ἀποδεδώκασι. ⌗15 discusses the differences between Rhetoric and Dialectics in a manner to show a sharp realization of the viewpoint of the allied art. Cf. Rabe, *op. cit.*

ἀνάγεται, some of them will list the item, ἐπὶ ποῖον εἶδος τῆς ῥητορικῆς ἀνάγεται,[9] and they handle this item in a fashion that clearly shows their dependence on the philosophers. Others again will say that they are going to change the last point in their enumeration, and, instead of ποῖον μέρος τῆς φιλοσοφίας ἀνάγεται, they will treat of διὰ τί προτετίμηται τῶν ἄλλων ὁ 'Αφθόνιος τῶν περὶ ῥητορικῶν προγυμνασμάτων διαλαβόντων.[10] As further proof of their knowledge of the philosophers, we have the fact that several of these anonymous works will, after they have discussed the items of their introduction, mention that other points might be included and then will treat briefly of ποῖον μέρος τῆς φιλοσοφίας ἀνάγεται and also of τὸν χαρακτῆρα τοῦ βιβλίου.[11]

The last item, ὁ χαρακτήρ, is said to be threefold, ἁδρός, μέσος and ταπεινός, the three traditional styles of a piece of oratorical writing.[12] This latter is the only specifically rhetorical item added by these commentators. They also, like the philosophers, imply that this introductory technique is of obligation for every commentator in the rhetorical field.[13] It is further interesting that some of them, when they treat of ποῖον μέρος τῆς φιλοσοφίας, will merely mention that their work comes under the field of Logic and refer us to the philosophers for a detailed treatment of the controversy as to whether Logic is a μέρος τῆς φιλοσοφίας or merely an ὄργανον.[14]

It is striking that the rhetoricians also have concocted ten questions as a form of introduction to some of their commentaries. The labored character of these ten points leads me to believe that they were invented in imitation of the analogous framework of the philosophers.[15] There is an apparent straining

---

240–241, as follows: 'Επεὶ οὖν ἀποδέδεικται οὖσα ἡ ῥητορική, ἄξιον εἰπεῖν, τίνι διαφέρει τῆς διαλεκτικῆς, κατὰ τὸ εἶδος αὐτῇ κοινωνοῦσα: λογικαὶ γὰρ ἄμφω. διαφέρουσι δ'οὖν ἀλλήλων πρῶτον μὲν τῇ ὕλῃ . . . ἔπειτα τοῖς ὀργάνοις . . . ἔτι διαφέρουσι καὶ τῷ τέλει . . . τετάρτη διαφορὰ ἡ ἀπὸ τοῦ τόπου . . . τινὲς δὲ προστιθέασι καὶ ἄλλας δύο διαφοράς. . . . #27 in treating of the last topic finally claims Rhetoric as a branch of Logic, and in so many words, refrains from discussing the question of the relation of Logic to Philosophy. It seems probable from a cursory reading of much of the literature on this topic that the relations between the two arts of Rhetoric and Dialectics were very close, and that the rhetoricians had practically adopted the manner of treatment of the Logicians.

9 Rabe, op. cit. 293, 9–13 and infra, p. 46 n. 21.

10 Rabe, op. cit. 79, 8–17 and infra, p. 46 n. 19.

11 Rabe, op. cit. 373, 1–13.

12 This latter topic is the traditional division of styles into genus sublime, medium et humile, traditional among the Rhetoricians since Aristotle.

13 Thus, Rabe #9 Johannis Doxapatris in Aphthonii Progymnasmata 127, 22–25 refers to these topics as 'the points so often talked about': 'Ελθωμεν λοιπὸν καὶ ἐπὶ τὴν τῶν πολυθρυλήτων κεφαλαίων ζήτησιν ὀκτὼ τὸν ἀριθμόν, ὥς φασι, τυγχανόντων. ἔστι δὲ ταῦτα ὁ σκοπός, κτλ. Rabe, #13, 244, 9: ἐπὶ παντὸς δὲ βιβλίου καὶ μάλιστα τεχνικοῦ. . . Rabe, #17, 288, 9: ταῦτα γὰρ ἐν παντὶ συγγράμματι ζητητέον. Rabe, #20, 304, 4–6; 360, 9–11; and especially, 401, 27–29: φέρε τὰ πρὸ παντὸς κανονιστικοῦ βιβλίου λήμματα προζητήσωμεν, ἅ εἰσιν ὁ σκοπός κτλ.

14 Rabe, op. cit. 317, 8–11: 'Αναφέρεται δὲ καὶ τὸ παρὸν βιβλίον ὑπὸ τὸ λογικὸν τῆς φιλοσοφίας, ὅπερ εἴτε μέρος ἐστὶν αὐτῆς εἴτε ὄργανον, τοῖς ἐξηγουμένοις τὴν λογικὴν τοῦ 'Αριστοτέλους πραγματείαν ἐντυχὼν ἀκριβέστερον εἴσῃ.

15 Thus they ask whether Rhetoric is from the gods; was it used by the 'heroes'; how did it come to mankind; why did it reach its peak at Athens; definition of rhetoric, forms of

after the magical number of ten, and they do not include (as did the philosophers) the technique of the *accessus* within this framework, but it is found as an independent form of *prooemium*. Some of these commentators make use of the fourfold form of inquiry taken from Aristotle, but there is no evidence of a close alliance between this and the seven or eight points of our technique.[16]

The adjoining chart of the use of the *schema* in which we are interested will show how closely the rhetoricians adhered to the traditional form of introduction. The numbers at the head of each column are those of the *prolegomena* published by Rabe. The numbers directly below each of these indicate the order in which the items appear in each of the commentators. The roman numerals at the bottom of each column are the suggested dates (in centuries) for each work, as given by Rabe. On this latter point it is proper to point out that Rabe's reasons for choosing these dates are sometimes quite arbitrary,

THE ACCESSUS AMONG THE RHETORICIANS

Rabe, *Proleg. Syll.*	8	9	11	13	15	17	20	27	28	32	33
ὁ σκοπός	1	1	1	1	1	1	1	1	1	1	1
τὸ χρήσιμον	2	2	2	2	2	2	2	2	2	2	2
τὸ γνήσιον	3	3	3	3	4	3	3	3	4	3	3
ἡ τάξις	4	4	4	4	5	4	4	4	5	5	4
ἡ ἐπιγραφή	5	5	5	5	3	6	5	5	3	4	5
ἡ διαίρεσις	6	6	6	—	6	—	6	6	6	7	6
ὁ διδασκαλικὸς τρόπος	7	7	7	—	—	5	7	7	—	6	7
διὰ τί Ἀφθ. τῶν ἄλλων προτετίμηται	8	8	—	—	—	—	—	—	—	—	—
ποῖον μέρος τῆς φιλοσοφίας	(9)	(9)	8	—	—	—	8	9	—	8	8
ποῖον εἶδος τῆς ῥητορικῆς	—	—	—	6	—	7	—	—	—	—	—
ὁ χαρακτήρ	(10)	(10)	—	—	—	—	—	8	—	—	—
Probable dates	V–VI	XI	XI	X	VI	?	?	XI	VI	XI	XI

and in the case of those assigned to early centuries, there might be some doubt as to their correctness.[17] However, an exact date is not essential to our pur-

rhetoric, the number of rhetoricians, kinds of rhetorical treatises, kinds of civil constitutions, and how many ways of rhetorical exegesis are used by rhetoricians. The development of this last topic is unlike the *schema* we have been studying; he claims the rhetorical commentator may handle his matter: κατὰ ἀλληγορίαν, κατὰ προϋφήγησιν, κατὰ ἱστορίαν, κατὰ σχῆμα, κατὰ ἰδέαν, κατὰ τέχνην, κατὰ σαφήνειαν (Rabe, 41–42). As to the origin of these ten questions, Rabe says: 'In medio relinquo, utrum interpretes rhetorici schema X capitum constituerint an philosophici, certe eodem consilio ab utrisque adhibitum est: ut decas efficeretur' (*Praefatio*, v). From a careful study of these ten topics in the rhetoricians and the philosophers, I believe that the framework erected by the latter gives evidence of greater solidity and less of a mere desire to construct a series of ten questions.

16 Aristotle, *Anal. Post.* 89b 23.

17 Rabe, *op. cit.* xlvii, cvii–cix. Thus from the fact that one of these commentators speaks very highly of Porphyry, he concludes that it must have been written not much later

pose, as it seems clear that all of them are dependent on the Aristotelian commentators of the sixth and seventh centuries.

The opening section of the anonymous *Prolegomena in Aphthonii Progymnasmata* is as follows:

Ζητητέον καὶ ἐπὶ τῆς ῥητορικῆς τὰ ὀκτὼ κεφάλαια, ἐστὶ δὲ ταῦτα· ὁ σκοπός, τὸ χρήσιμον, τὸ γνήσιον, ἡ τάξις, ἡ αἰτία τῆς ἐπιγραφῆς, ἡ εἰς τὰ μόρια διαίρεσις, ὁ διδασκαλικὸς τρόπος, καὶ ἀντὶ τῆς ὑπὸ τί μέρος ἀναφορᾶς, ἥτις ἐν τοῖς κατὰ φιλοσοφίαν ὡς ἐπὶ τὸ πολὺ εἴωθε ζητεῖσθαι συγγράμμασι, διὰ τί προτετίμηται ὁ Ἀφθόνιος τῶν περὶ ῥητορικῶν προγυμνασμάτων διαλαβόντων.[18]

Each one of these points is thereafter developed at considerable length and the meaning of each is the same as among the philosophers. As the last item he mentions is a new one, it will be helpful to have before us his complete account of this heading.

Ὄγδοον κεφάλαιον, διὰ τί τὰ τοῦ Ἀφθονίου Προγυμνάσματα τῶν Ἑρμογένους καὶ τῶν λοιπῶν προτετίμηται· καὶ φαμεν, ὡς σαφέστερα τῶν ἄλλων καὶ εὐληπτότερα. ὁ μὲν γὰρ Ἑρμογένης καὶ οἱ λοιποὶ μεθόδους ψιλὰς χωρὶς παραδειγμάτων ἐκθέμενοι δυσχερῆ τὴν τῶν προγυμνασμάτων πραγματείαν τοῖς εἰσαγομένοις ἐποίησαν, ὁ δὲ Ἀφθόνιος οὐ μόνον τὰς μεθόδους ὡς ἐνῆν σαφῶς καὶ διηρθρωμένως ποιήσας, ἀλλὰ καὶ παραδείγμασι φωτίσαι βουληθεὶς τὰ λεγόμενα προσφυέστερος τοῖς νέοις καὶ οἰκειότερος ἔδοξε.[19]

At the conclusion of his treatment of these eight points, the author mentions that some writers will also include *pars philosophiae* and the particular style of the work, as has been referred to above. The text of these short paragraphs follows:

Τινὲς δὲ καὶ τὴν ὑπὸ τί μέρος ἀναφορὰν καὶ ἐπὶ τοῦ παρόντος βιβλίου ζητοῦντες ἀναφέρεσθαί φασιν αὐτὸ οὔτε εἰς τὸ θεωρητικόν, ἐπειδὴ μὴ φυσιολογεῖ ἢ θεολογεῖ ἢ μαθηματικεύεται, ἀλλ᾽ οὐδὲ εἰς τὸ πρακτικόν—οὐδὲ γὰρ πῶς δεῖ κοσμεῖν τὰ ἤθη διδάσκει—, ἀλλ᾽ εἰς τὸ μέσον τούτων μεθοδικὸν καὶ ὀργανικόν, ἔστι δὲ τοῦτο τὸ λογικόν· κανόνας γὰρ καὶ μεθόδους διδάσκει.

Τινὲς δὲ καὶ τὸν χαρακτῆρα ζητοῦσιν, εἰσὶ δὲ τρεῖς, ἀδρός, ταπεινός, μέσος· ἀδρὸς μὲν ὁ κομπηρὰς ἔχων λέξεις, νοῦν δὲ ταπεινόν, ὡς ἔχει τὰ τοῦ Λυκόφρονος· ταπεινὸς δὲ ὁ νοῦν μὲν ἔχων ὑψηλόν, λέξεις δὲ ταπεινάς, ὡς τὰ τοῦ θεολόγου· μέσος δὲ ὁ μήτε νοῦν ἔχων ὑψηλὸν μήτε λέξεις κομπηράς, ἀλλ᾽ ἀμφότερα μέτρια, οἷά εἰσιν ὡς ἐπὶ τὸ πλεῖστον τὰ τοῦ Χρυσοστόμου. χρῆται δὲ ὁ Ἀφθόνιος καὶ τοῖς τρισί, τῷ μὲν ἀδρῷ ἐν τῇ ἠθοποιίᾳ, τῷ ἀνειμένῳ καὶ ταπεινῷ ἐν τῇ ἐκφράσει, τῷ δὲ μέσῳ ἔν τισι τῶν ἄλλων.[20]

---

than the fifth century (78, 1). This would seem to imply that there was a lapse in the knowledge of Porphyry and his work, a conclusion that is hardly tenable, in view of the frequency of commentary many centuries after his time.

[18] Rabe, *op. cit.* ≠ 8, 73, 11–17.
[19] Rabe, *op. cit.* ≠ 8, 79, 8–17.
[20] Rabe, *op. cit.* ≠ 8, 79, 18–80, 7.
[21] Rabe, *op. cit.* ≠ 17, 293, 9–13.

The last item of interest is that of ἐπὶ ποῖον εἶδος τῆς ῥητορικῆς, the treatment of which is rather brief, as follows :

Λείπεται δὲ ἄρα διδάξαι, ἐπὶ ποῖον εἶδος τῆς ῥητορικῆς ἀνάγεται ἡ παροῦσα τέχνη. λέγομεν οὖν ἐπὶ τὸ δικανικὸν καὶ συμβουλευτικόν· τὸ γὰρ παʹηγυρικὸν ἀστασίαστόν ἐστιν, ἐπειδὴ ὁμολογουμένων ἀγαθῶν ἐστιν αὔξησις.[21]

V. CONCLUSION

Thus we have seen that the practice of the *accessus* was prominently used by the commentators on medieval *grammatica, rhetorica* and *dialectica* and in both civil and canon law. In the twelfth and thirteenth centuries, it was also used in theology, scriptural exegesis,[1] and in philosophical works.[2] It is to be found in the famous letter of Dante to Can Grande della Scala, which explains the *Divina Commedia,*[3] and a striking example is to be found in a thirteenth-century work in French, in which it appears not in a commentary, but in the opening section of a poem of Peter of Peckham, *La Lumière as Lais.*[4] This writer has not investigated the field of commentaries on the *quadrivium* and it is likely

---

[1] Beryl Smalley, *The Study of the Bible in the Middle Ages* (Oxford 1941) 74: 'After a short prologue Hugh [of St. Victor] summarizes the various kinds of sacrifice prescribed in Leviticus, the persons who are to offer, the times and the seasons. This is not quite equivalent to the usual prologue, known as *accessus* or *materia*, with its *causa scribendi, materia, intentio* which was common to the grammarians, the theologians, and the lawyers.' From this statement, I infer that the practice of an *accessus* was not notably developed among the exegetes. In any case, it would not seem that its use in that field or among the theologians is of great significance for the origins of the practice. Abailard in his *Commentariorum super S. Pauli Epistolam ad Romanos libri quinque* (PL 178, 785–786) speaks of *Intentio generalis omnium epistolarum* and of *intentiones propriae [singularum epistolarum], materia* and *modus tractandi.* Thierry of Chartres in his *De sex dierum operibus* mentions *intentio, utilitas, titulus;* cf. B. Hauréau, *Notices et extraits de quelques manuscrits latins de la bibliothèque nationale* I (Paris 1890) 52, citing from Paris B.N. lat. 647, (saec. XII). Cf. A. Wilmart, *Codices Vaticani Reginenses*, pp. 118 [*Vat. Reg. lat.* 50, fol. 77ᵛ] and 176 [*Vat. Reg. lat.* 79, fol. 74ʳ], both of the twelfth century.

[2] Petri Abaelardi *Glossae super Porphyrium* (ed. B. Geyer, Beiträge zur Geschichte der Philosophie des Mittelalters, XXI, 1, 2, Münster 1919, pp. 2 and 111–113) has *intentio, materia, modus tractandi, utilitas, per quam partem logicae.* . . . This work is a commentary on Boethius and hence it is clear whence Abailard took at least this use of the technique. Cf. also V. Cousin, *Oeuvres inédits d'Abélard* (Paris 1848) 608. W. Jansen, *Der Kommentar des Clarenbaldus von Arras zu Boethius De Trinitate, Ein Werk aus der Schule von Chartres im 12. Jahrhundert* (Breslau 1926) 3*, a work which purports to be a complete edition of the MSS, strangely omits three folia. Thus, fol. 66ʳ: 'Librum hunc de Trinitate inchoantibus primo videndum est, quae sit auctoris intentio, quae libri utilitas, ad quem scribat . . . [fol. 69ʳ] Christianae religionis. etc. . . .' From the length of the indicated gap, it would appear that this is a rather substantial prologue and its omission is somewhat hard to understand.

[3] 'Sex igitur sunt quae in principio cuiusque doctrinalis operis inquirenda sunt, videlicet subiectum, agens, forma, finis, libri titulus et genus philosophiae.' *Le Opere di Dante, Testo Critico della Società Dantesca Italiana* (Firenze 1921) *Ep.* XIII, 436.

[4] Cf. P. Meyer, 'Les manuscrits français de Cambridge' (cod. St. Johns F. 30), *Romania*

that traces of the practice could be discovered there as well.[5]　However, there is nothing that leads me to suspect that its use in that field would go back beyond that of the philosophers and hence, the possibility could not influence our judgment as to the original source of the practice.　It seems clear that in the twelfth century the tremendous growth of interest in the studies of Antiquity led to the extension of a practice that had been a tradition, apparently dormant in some fields for centuries, and totally unknown in others.　Further researches in this and later centuries might lead to additional examples of the use of the technique which by that time had become a commonplace of the schools.

It is clear from some of the twelfth- and thirteenth-century examples that the stream of the tradition had run its course.　The details of the *accessus* had, to some extent, become shadowy and dim, and we see merely the survival of a practice that had largely lost its real meaning.[6]　Of all the later practitioners, those in the field of law alone seem to have made good use of it.　Among the lawyers, it was a source of inspiration and a stimulus to speculative thinking along lines that were of value in the development of juristic science.

The only field in which the practice certainly goes back to the fifth or sixth centuries, is that of Dialectics, and specifically, to the commentaries on the logical and other works of Aristotle.　It is found full-blown in the works of the school of Ammonius, and traces are seen in the work of Proclus, Porphyry and Alexander Aphrodisias.　The loss of most of the works of this last, the greatest of the commentators, is a serious obstacle to a further tracing of the practice. The present state of the evidence, however, shows us that a practice, found in rudimentary form in Alexander, is completely developed in the work of commentators who leaned heavily on him for many of their ideas.　The remark of Elias, to the effect that, in using it, he is following the behest, or perhaps merely

---

VIII (Paris 1879).　This work of Peter of Peckham is said to be a vernacular adaptation of the *Elucidarium* of Honorius of Autun, in which he tells us:

> Cinc choses sunt en ja enquere
> Au commencement en liver fere:
> Ki fut autur e l'entitlement
> E la matire e la furme ensement,
> E la fin, par quei ceo est resun
> Fu fete la composiciun (487–492).

He then continues in some detail on each one of the points and makes a distinction between 'une fin générale . . . e une autre espéciale.' The entrance of the technique of the *accessus* into the vernacular in the thirteenth century is, perhaps, the final goal of this practice that had come so far over the centuries.　Pierpont Morgan MS M.761 (saec. xiii ex.) contains a complete text of this work.

[5] Boethius' works on mathematics, mainly translations from Nicomachus, show no indication of its use in that field.　It is very probable that his interest in mathematics preceded his work on Porphyry and Aristotle, and hence it may be suggested that he did not become acquainted with the *accessus* until he turned to the philosophers.

[6] This is not to imply that the practice was completely sterile in the twelfth century. The use of the technique could have been a stimulating and effective school practice even though the students were unaware of the steps whereby they were constrained to decide where in the field of philosophy they should locate the works of Ovid or Lucan.

the suggestion of Proclus, cannot be substantiated from the extant works of that author.

The ultimate source and invention of this stylized form of introduction, then, certainly goes back to the Greek philosophical commentators. It seems evident that the Greek rhetoricians took its use from the Aristotelian commentators. The Latin rhetoricians do not manifest any acquaintance with it in its proper form and our knowledge of the sources of their rhetorical information do not indicate any connection with the Greeks.[7] The only Latin student of philosophy who certainly had direct contact with Greek thought was Boethius and his influence in spreading the practice in the West can hardly be over-estimated. There is strong probability that Boethius influenced the writers on Law and he may have been the direct instrument of its entrance into that field. The popularity of his commentary on the *Isagoge* of Porphyry was certainly widespread all through the Middle Ages among those who were interested in Logic, and, certainly in the twelfth century, as in the case of Abailard, Boethius was the dominant influence.[8] There is no doubt of the extraordinary extension of the *accessus* in that century; there is strong probability that Boethius was the source from which knowledge of the *accessus* came to that century.

The presence of the *accessus* in the schools of dialectic and of rhetoric in the early centuries of the Middle Ages in the East would allow us to presume that it was also found in the schools of grammar. In the West, we find it in Boethius and in Donatus and Servius and it may also have been a tradition of the Roman schools of the Later Empire, since we know of no Greek influence on the two latter writers. That it was not, apparently, an 'obligatory' practice in the West seems clear from the fact that no line of tradition developed from their use of it. Thus St. Jerome, a pupil of Donatus, makes no use of it in the prefaces to his commentaries on the various books of the Bible.[9] Further, although both Donatus and Servius were known in the ninth century, its presence in their works does not seem to have had any appreciable influence at that time. This, however, may be so because of the comparative lack of commentatorial activity in that period. The preoccupation with merely preserving the resources of the past, so strong at that time, might have inhibited the attempt at original commentary, which actually came later, under the influence of the pronounced stirrings of intellectual interest of the twelfth century.

In the variations of the practice over the course of centuries, we catch a glimpse of the scholarly interests of our forebears. We see men who set about

---

[7] W. H. D. Suringar, *Historia critica scholiastarum latinorum* (Lyon 1854) I, 213, published a 'Fragmentum scholiastae inediti ad Ciceronem De Inventione Rhetorica,' to which he assigns a date very close to that of Boethius, on evidence that seems to me to be rather scanty.

[8] The personal popularity of Abailard in the schools of Paris and his use of this technique in his lectures would have been a potent means of spreading the acquaintance with this form of prologue, among students of the twelfth century.

[9] Cf. Ignatius S. Kozik, 'St. Jerome's Biblical Preface' (unpub. M.A. thesis, Fordham University, 1938).

their task of explaining the learning of the past in serious and systematic fashion.   Perhaps, from our viewpoint, they are picayune in their love for detail and *schematismus*.   However, the elaborate structure they erected is testimony to their vigor of mind and inventiveness.   The man who invented this comprehensive technique of the *accessus* was undoubtedly a trail-blazer in his day and he must have dreamed, as has every serious scholar, of making a lasting contribution to the store of learning and to the science and art of teaching.   He has done his work well.